DREAM SELFIE

DREAM SELFIE

REFLECTIONS OF THE INNER I

by

MICHAEL KLEIN

KINGBIRD CREATIVE
TORONTO * 2021

CONTENTS

PREFACE

BOOK MISSION: i) To probe the nature of dreams, ii) To provide a comprehensive method for interpreting and working with your own dreams.

THE PREMISES OF THIS WORK ARE AS FOLLOWS:

> Only the dreamer can fully understand their own dreams. A dream therapist or guide can only point the way – ultimately, only the dreamer knows the true and complete meaning of their own dreams.

> Owning a dream is empowering and therefore can bring about healing and personal growth.

The goal of this work is to provide a practical guide to interpreting one's own dreams. I have also offered herein a very brief, historical overview of dream interpretation and dream healing. From this overview the reader will come to appreciate the root sources which, woven together, provide the foundation of our **DREAM-SELFIE** methodology. As a primary tool for interpreting my own dreams and to help others do the same, the Dream-Selfie method is based on a synthesis of approaches and techniques ancient and modern, and many years of meticulous research and self-examination.

This guide to interpreting one's own dreams is, in part, an eclectic fusion of various, psychodynamic approaches that branched out from the ground-breaking theories of Freud and Jung in the early 20th century, and from subsequent, scientific, clinical and laboratory research. These modern approaches themselves have evolved from understandings that reach back to ancient and even primitive human cultures.

When taken together, all the scientific data, clinical methodology and mystic inspiration, have provided dynamic guidance and shed some light on our understanding. And yet, the true nature of dreams ultimately remains a mystery and perhaps always shall. Only through direct experience can one draw close to the mystery of one's own dream life. I urge you dear reader to incorporate your own dream life experiences to the application of this work, because, when it comes to understanding your own dreams, you are the expert

– ONLY YOU!

2021

PART I
WORLD OF DREAMS

INTRODUCTION: A WORLD OF OUR OWN

Dreams have always been a part of human life. In the pages ahead we will see the many functional ways that they have impacted our world. Their retelling, embedded in folk cultures around the world, dreams have shaped much of the world's mythology. They have been the cornerstone of religions and are a prominent theme in every known faith system. They have been the celestial signifier testifying to the divine selection of Emperors and Kings. Dreams have also been the harbinger of culture-transforming, technological advances. They have been the inspiration behind numerous works of art, as well as many scientific discoveries. From prehistoric times until the present day people have been using dreams to heal and guide individuals and whole social groups. In the classical Greco-Roman world, healers used dream incubation and interpretation as a primary treatment for a variety of diseases, especially those with psychosomatic symptoms. Classical and medieval physicians used dreams as diagnostic tools. Freud and his numerous, Depth-Psychology inheritors redefined the age-old practices of using dreams to heal psychological disorders. More recently, developmental psychologists have traced a strong functional connection between dreaming and learning. We will see that, as an outlet for repressed human impulses, dreams provide a healing function, in and of themselves, even when we don't recall, interpret or analyze them. In all these ways dreams have been a functional part of human culture and of our lives, and yet there remains an even more basic, nonetheless inscrutable aspect of dreaming – one that encompasses all of the above – **our interpersonal relationship with ourselves.** In the physical world we cannot see our own face without a mirror; dreams are the mirror of our souls. They are among the most intimate of our human experiences, providing a corridor to a supernal world; a world where magic, myth, prophecy and sacred vigor become manifest reality; a world of our own. Spiritual aspirants from many mystical traditions seek to connect to their essential being through a variety of methods, including prayer, meditation, physical exercises, vision-quests, drug-induced trances, ritual dancing, chanting, ritual sacrifices, fasting, feasting and the list goes on. People go to extreme lengths to achieve some sort of transcendental experience, often overlooking the spiritual connection that occurs naturally, each night as we sleep. Dreams are everyday miracles.

Throughout history and into present times there have been those who insist that dreams are meaningless. This position cannot be disproven or proven because dreams are, essentially, mystical experiences. As such, they are experiences that are ultimately beyond the reach of empirical research, and only the dreamer can know if they are meaningful or not. Finding meaning in a dream is, in part, an experience that requires a super-rational leap into a mystical dimension. It's not that the dream itself is super-rational – indeed, most often, when dream symbols are accurately decoded they usually convey a coherent, rational message – but, rather, it is the mystical understanding of the source of dreams that requires a leap. A great sage of olden day once said *"a journey of 500 miles begins with a single step."* But the first step is not easy; separating one's foot from the ground is vital, and up to each of us to take that first action.

Only the dreamer can know the
true meaning of their dreams.

CHAPTER ONE

THE NATURE OF DREAMS

WE ALL DREAM

Although dreams can never be fully understood in the context of clinical science, work in modern labs has established two irrefutable and important facts: 1) We all dream, and 2) Dreaming is a functional aspect of human physiological and psychological life.

Scientific studies have shown that we all do dream regularly (except for some very rare exceptions). Now, many of us will say that we do not remember dreams or that we dream very rarely, but numerous, solid, sleep studies have shown that, on average, people dream at least four or five times per seven hour sleep. Most people spend about one third of their lives asleep and, at least, one quarter of their sleep-time dreaming. Although we often don't remember, every one of us will spend many years of our lives in the world of dreams.

WHAT IS A DREAM?

Scientific research has shown that dreaming is certainly a universal process, active in the life of all human beings. We know that dreaming is a primary, autonomic process, as are breathing and digestion, which are part of normal, human, physiological functioning. Researchers have been able to tell us much about the physiology of dreams, but just what a dream is and why we dream remain elusive questions. Dreams happen in a private world that cannot be probed by any scientist or technical instrument. Laboratory researchers can tell us much about the biological, neurological and physical processes that accompany dream states. They can monitor changes in our heart-rate and breathing as we enter a dream phase of sleep, and they can even show us detailed pictures of our electrical, brain activity as we dream. Clinical work can identify physical processes that occur during dream-states, like rapid eye movement and sexual arousal. In an experimental setting, sleep-scientists have also been able to study the detrimental effects of dream deprivation. By waking and immediately questioning dreaming subjects during different dream/sleep states, researchers have even been able to trace patterns in the qualities and subject matter of dreams. But, of course, these are merely reflections and shadows of this ubiquitous and vital human phenomenon. Dreams will always defy definition and categorization. They will always remain essentially mysterious. Although dreaming is a universal phenomenon, dreams are among our most personal experiences, borne in an inner world unique to each dreamer. To learn more, each dreamer must leave the laboratory and venture into the field – the field of our own hearts and minds.

I broadly define dreaming herein as **the awakening of consciousness while the body sleeps.** Occasionally the dreamer is conscious of themselves, as an observer, watching the dream unfold as if one is viewing a movie. At other times, especially with some vivid dreams, the dreamer is, not merely a spectator, but fully involved in the dream experience. In the most powerful dreams the dreamer is both witness and participant. When this simultaneous spectator/participant experience occurs, the dreamer's perception is transposed toward an elevated consciousness. This type of dream provides opportunity for profound self-cognizance and even spiritual transformation.

WHY WE DREAM

Science and common knowledge have shown that dreaming is certainly a universal process, active in the life of all human beings. Dreaming may be viewed, at least in part, as a function of our nervous systems. Like the circulatory system, the respiratory system and the digestive system, the nervous system operates primarily through autonomic processes. These processes are ongoing and usually unconscious unless they malfunction. They are essential to survival and well-being.

Human-biologists have come a long way in the study of the operations of our various physiological systems. Through observation, physiologists have been able to determine the specific jobs of particular, body organs and or processes. On a mechanical level, we know how the heart works; we know how the stomach, kidneys and intestines function; we know the exact purposes of many elements within each physiological system; but, when it comes to dreams, we have only incidental, physical evidence and indirect, imaginative experience to draw from. As to the primary functions of dreams, despite some discerning theories, we must rely on intuition and conjecture to provide some compelling insights. Once again, various ideas about the functions of dreams may each offer a valid perspective, not necessarily mutually exclusive, because dreams are multi-dimensional and multi-functional.

The earliest, human traditions viewed dreams as **a means of connecting with the divine or spiritual world** and, for many even today, this remains the primary function of dreams.

Many psychologists view dreaming as a sort of safety valve, providing a free-space where one can cathartically satisfy primal wishes and desires without the constraints of social norms or conscious censoring. Satisfying our unconscious desires in dreams prevents them from impinging inappropriately in our waking lives.

In Jungian and other psychodynamic schools of thought, dreams are purposeful guides in a process of self realization. In the realm of dreams we can confront our deepest hopes and fears on a personal journey towards wholeness.

For many depth psychologists dreams function as a gateway to an individual's unconscious, which helps with diagnosing the sources of psychological disorders and provides a path towards healing.

Some cognitive psychologists have done quantitative studies suggesting that the dreaming mind functions like a sorter/editor, computer application, that processes each day's events as we sleep, sifting, organizing saving and discarding data.

In addition to organizing our psychic data the dreaming mind may also function to solve problems, resolve conflicts and make decisions based on the data it has received. As per the common adage, *"I think I'll sleep on it"*.

Scientific studies have also shown that dreaming facilitates learning and that dream deprivation has negative effects on our psychological functioning, but just how and why these processes operate remains elusive.

It's worth noting that many theorists, both ancient and modern, have claimed that the content of dreams is, in fact, meaningless, not subject to interpretation and should best be ignored. The idea that some dreams are meaningless and possibly misleading was expressed hundreds of years ago by the medieval, Sephardic, scholar/physician Abarabnel. He writes that *"dreams are the revelation of disorganized thoughts that are suppressed during waking hours and released during sleep. Such dreams are vain, have no meaning and have no effect one way or the other."*

In modern times also, dreams are sometimes viewed as mere empty scraps of thought or electrical discharge that fizzles within our brains as we sleep. In 1983 two American scientists, Francis Crick and Graeme Mitchison, wrote an influential paper, entitled <u>The Function of Dreams</u>. By meticulous observation of electrical activity in the brain, they developed the theoretical idea that the function of dreaming was to cleanse the mind of mental waste – sort of like a mental bowel-movement. *"We propose that the function of dream sleep (more properly rapid-eye movement or REM sleep) is to remove certain undesirable modes of interaction in networks of cells in the cerebral cortex. We postulate that this is done in REM sleep by a reverse learning mechanism, so that the trace in the brain of the unconscious dream is weakened, rather than strengthened, by the dream."*

According to this theory, the process of dreaming is important in order to clear the mind; however the actual dream content was viewed as being meaningless. With the expansion of neurophysiologic studies, some researchers focus on form as opposed to content when considering dreams. Their view postulates that dreams are primarily reflections of physiologic conditions in the sleeping brain. The bizarre images that often appear in dreams are attributed to a state of disorientation that occurs during sleep, rather than as meaningful, symbolic representations. Although I strongly disagree with those who adhere to a strictly physiological understanding of dreaming, I take their words as a cautionary note – applying erroneous meanings to dreams can be dangerously misleading.

THE PARADOX OF DREAM EXPERIENCE

Dreams may be pleasurable or painful, uplifting or depressing, comforting or frightening. Dreams are experiences, and like any experience they have an impact on the person, even if the person has forgotten the experience. Unlike experiences that occur in the physical world, dreams, which occur in a world created by the psychic energy of the dreamer, do not impact the material world directly, except for a few exceptions; but they do affect the material world indirectly. I once had a dream that one of my hands had been cut off, but, of course, upon awakening in a palpitating panic, I was relieved to find that my hand was still there. After a few, brief moments I was able to brush off the negative memory of the dream – after all it was only a dream. I understood that the dream was not real. It did not really happen, at least on a physical level. And yet, I did experience my hand being severed. Although my hand was not actually cut off, my body was directly impacted by fear and panic. This is the paradox of dream experience – It happens and yet it does not happen. How is the dreamer affected by such an experience? When a cigarette smoker, in withdrawal, dreams of smoking are they actually satisfying a powerful need, which in turn impacts on the dreamer's physical body? When a starving person dreams of eating does the dream meal have any effect on the dreamer's digestive system? What is the dynamic relation between the physical world and the dream world? We know that the two worlds, material and psychic, are separate yet interconnected. For example, if I have an erotic dream, my heartbeat and breathing will quicken as if I was actually engaging in sexual activity. I might even experience full, ejaculate orgasm, directly impacting my body. Erotic dreams may also satisfy, or mollify emotional and psychological needs, indirectly interfacing with our waking reality. Even when we don't recall them, our dreams still do their work. They can help quench the fire of desire without the dangers of an actual, inappropriate or dangerous encounter. Because they lack direct consequences in the waking world, dreams are a safe place to work things out, to experiment and to release pent-up emotions.

WHY INTERPRET DREAMS?

If you rarely recall your dreams and have no real interest in interpreting your dreams, then don't bother. Healthy dreaming functions, in your life, in a preconscious or unconscious fashion, as do other autonomic processes in our bodies like breathing, digestion or cellular regeneration. Except for routine medical check-ups, we usually don't analyze these processes unless we perceive a problem. When some mal-function inhibits the proper performance of these systems, symptoms of disease occur. When we consciously experience symptoms, such as pain, fatigue, flatulence etc., we generally recognize that it's time to analyze the source of the symptom in order to take steps to correction. So it is with dreams. As a primary autonomic function of the sleeping body, dreaming usually operates without the dreamer being conscious of these processes. However, as with other autonomic processes, sometimes there is a malfunction that may produce symptoms of negative emotions and behaviors; what Freud called ***"neurosis"*** and ***"psychosis"***. When we become aware of such symptoms, dreams are often our best and most direct avenue for analyzing and thereby dealing with the problem. Simply put, if a person is experiencing unexplained or partially understood emotions or behaviors, then recalling and analyzing their dreams is an invaluable tool that can help identify the source of a problem. In some cases dreams themselves can become symptoms, as with recurring nightmares. Understanding bad dreams is the best way to make them stop. When someone is feeling anxious or depressed or any other negative emotion, without understanding the source of their feelings, it is their recent dreams that will lead them directly to core issues and conflicts that are generating the negative emotions. Once a discomfiting issue is brought to light, one can begin to consciously resolve the conflicts. For our purposes dreams are an effective tool. Their function is to provide us with self-knowledge. As the sages throughout the ages, from Pythagoras to Freud, have reiterated, ***"know thyself"***. Self knowledge is liberating and empowering and healing.

Even when one is not aware of negative symptoms, when a dream, especially a recurring dream, is recalled with a sense of apprehension disturbance, deep intrigue or even profound curiosity, then rest assured that interpretation will be fruitful. According to the ancient Babylonian Talmud *"a dream not interpreted is like a letter unread."* Most of us have, in fact, experienced a dream that hung around with us all day, somehow calling to us, like a personal letter, from ourselves to ourselves, waiting to be opened.

I would be remiss if I failed to briefly mention some further, compelling reasons to recall and analyze dreams, aside from their function in psychological healing. Dreams remain a source of inspiration for artists and scientists alike, and one of humankind's deepest connections to the world of spirit. There are numerous, famous examples of creative thinkers, in both the sciences and the arts, who attribute a profound discovery to a dream. Exploring dreams is by no means confined to dealing with negative symptoms. For many there is a sense of joy and security that emanates from their dreams. Dreaming is often the progenitor of hope and spiritual awakening.

CHAPTER TWO
A BRIEF HISTORY OF DREAMS
HEALING, PROPHECY AND POLITICS

PRE-HISTORIC DREAMERS & SHAMANS

From earliest times dreams have been associated with healing and spirituality. When we look at the belief systems of primitive societies, we see that dreams and dreaming take central roles in the social order, religious practices and personal lives of individuals. Early humans lived within hunter-gathering societies, and followed a way of life very much like that of later primitive, tribal peoples. Anthropologists and archeologists have indentified hunter-gatherer societies, who walked the earth before the rise of agriculturally based civilizations over 12,000 years ago.

Primitive, tribal societies still exist today in small pockets around the globe on every continent, and include many of the aboriginal peoples of Australia and the Americas. For most of these, modern civilization has encroached upon the natural environment that is so intrinsic to their mode of living and sustenance. Most (a few scattered remnants remain) have had to change, being drawn into the pale of modern culture. But, despite a necessary shift into a different economic mode, many tribal peoples have retained elements of their spiritual traditions. The sacred practices of these different peoples have some remarkably similar features, despite wide variance of place and time. Dreams, in the context of almost all primitive, tribal societies are understood to be connected with the spirit world. Anthropologists usually refer to the spiritual practices or religion of most primitive peoples as **Shamanism,** because of the central, priest-like role played by the **Shaman**, the Medicine Man or Witchdoctor of common English parlance. The Shaman has the primary role as connector and intermediary between his people and the spirit world. He or she functions as a physician and spiritual healer for their group. Shamans ply their trade in a variety of ways including performing rituals and preparing and administering medicines. But their most important mode of healing is through the Shaman's power to connect with spirits in the spirit-world, or what Australian aborigines refer to as the ***"Dreamtime"***, the Nurumba of South Africa call the ***"Land of the Ancestors"***, the ancient Celts refer to as ***"Fairyland"*** and modern occultists call the ***"Astral Plane(s)"***.

Shamanic communication with the spirit world is usually done from within a lucid dream or a dream-like, trance state. The Shaman has the ability to induce this state of mind, while retaining cognizant consciousness, even though he may be physically prostrate. Sometimes the Shaman in trance will be sitting, sometimes lying down and sometimes dancing. Within this altered state there are several ways that the Shaman can connect with the spirit world. While in trance, Shamans may **allow spirits to temporarily possess their bodies**, so that a spirit being might speak or sing with the vocal chords of the Shaman. While in the trance-state the Shaman may act as a conduit to deliver a message directly to an individual or to a tribal assembly.

The Shaman may also experience **a vision,** like the visions of some of the biblical prophets. The vision will often carry a message in symbolic form and it is another of the Shaman's special skills to be able to interpret the symbolic language of the spirit realm.

Another possibility is that the Shaman will receive **a visitation from a spirit being.** The spirit being may appear in a natural form like a river, a mountain or a tree or, sometimes in the form of a human being, an animal, a hybrid or a supernatural being. The visitor might also be invisible, presenting as a disembodied voice. The visiting spirit will bring a message, a warning or a gift of wisdom, which the Shaman must obtain and bring back to the tribe. Often, but not always, the Shaman will be able to converse with the spirit.

While in the dream state a Shaman might also go on **a soul-journey** seeking gifts of knowledge, power and wisdom which can be brought back to the people in the waking world. The soul journey corresponds to the concept of astral projection in the modern, mystic traditions. It is understood that the Shaman's consciousness can travel within the spirit world in a subtle, astral body. This ethereal, energy body often takes the form of a beautiful animal or bird and the Shaman will experience lofty power and mobility. Occasionally the

Shaman may encounter evil spirits with which he will do battle in order to bring about a healing effect. The healing gifts that the Shaman seeks could pertain to the concerns of individuals, small groups or to the whole community – healing disease, locating better hunting and gathering grounds, understanding potentially disastrous weather and seasonal patterns, warnings about improper behavior and protection against attack from wild animals, demonic spirits or evil people.

The mythology, of early, tribal cultures, tells us that many of the technological advances, developed by prehistoric humans, came about as the result of gifts given by spirit beings, and these gifts were very often delivered in dreams. It was the earth itself that taught people how to live, through their dreams. A patent example, of this type of dream/myth from the First Nations of North America, tells how the people learnt about the cultivation of corn. There are many versions of this tale. Here is one, told to me personally by a Chipewyan, friend from the Lake Erie region: The tale relates how a spirit being, the beautiful corn maiden, appeared in a dream to a handsome young man whom she loved. The young man loved her in return but was tested when he was faced with the choice of leaving his people to marry the corn maiden in the spirit world, or remaining in his home world without her. When the young man chooses to sacrifice his earthly life for love, the corn maiden sacrifices herself instead, transforming into the magical corn plant. In the end the Corn maiden's spirit teaches the young hero how to plant and cultivate corn and how to use it for sustenance. The young man then shares the knowledge of corn cultivation with his people. Growing corn becomes a way of life. There are many other examples, even in modern times, where some profound technological or cultural innovation was engendered from a dream experience.

Many traditional, tribal societies have rites of passage for young men and women that are based on dreams. These rites mark a young person's transformation from childhood to adulthood as well as initiation into the tribal unit. A well-documented example, of a dream-based rite of passage, is the ***"Vision Quest"*** of the Blackfoot Cree from the American Plains. Young men are prepared with special (secret) training. They are informed with the ancestral mythology, transmitted orally by the shaman and elders and through artworks and songs. When the training is complete the young men are taken by tribal elders to a secluded area and are tasked with fasting and remaining perfectly still and awake. After 24hours, this process will induce a trancelike state in the inductees, during which they will invariably experience a vivid dream/vision. The young men are then brought back to the shaman and tribal elders where they report their vision. The Shaman will explain the vision and the young brave is ceremoniously given a new name by which he will be known for the rest of his adult life. The new name is based primarily on the dream/vision because it is believed that the vision reveals the true nature and personal direction of that individual. A name like *"Sitting Bull"* or *"Crazy Horse"* might sound simplistic but, in fact, these names contain deep psychological and social significance based on the dream-quests of these famous Native American chiefs.

ANCIENT DREAMS: PRIESTS AND POLITICS

About 12,000 years ago some of our pre-historic, hunter gatherer ancestors began to engage in agriculture and animal husbandry. Some remained semi-nomadic, slowly migrating with their herds in search of pasture. Others settled down near their fields. Technology advanced, writing emerges and recorded history was initiated. Eventually great cities and civilizations, with sophisticated, religious systems, emerged. Hunter-gatherer societies with tribal affiliations were eventually superseded by the rise of agriculturally-based communities, and these, in turn, developed into ancient, city-based cultures. Similar, cultural evolution occurred at different times and locations, around the world. Hunter-gatherer tribes continued to coexist around the edges and in the shadows of the great civilizations, preserving a lifestyle that is intimately tuned to the natural world around them. The emerging, ancient, city-based cultures gave rise to specialized, dream healers. The priests of Serapis in ancient Egypt, or the dream guides of Aesculapius in ancient Greece, were designated specialists who could interpret dreams, in some ways, not unlike many psychotherapists of modern day. Their purpose for interpreting dreams was to effect physical and, or emotional healing and also to facilitate an individual's, spiritual growth.

For mainstream civilization, spirit-beings, manifest within natural forces, were transformed into supernal gods. The role of the shaman, as the intermediary between the world of man and the world of spirits, was replaced by various forms of priesthood. The priestly role adopted an increasingly ritualistic character, with ceremony and sacrifice as the principal instruments for communicating with the gods. At the same time, the shamanistic function, meaning the direct communication with the spirit world in an altered state of consciousness, became less prevalent and often non-existent within the cultic bureaucracies of ancient city-states and empires. Dream-interpretation, in the framework of the ancient priesthoods, was reoriented towards divination, as were other practices like astrology, augury or numerology. An emphasis was placed on divination; the use of dreams to help decide future actions.

In the ancient world, interpretations and predictions were often politically motivated. Monarchs asserted their kingship, by divine right, as the chosen of the gods. Religion and dreams took, as a primary function, the affirmation of Kingship and political power. Sometimes the ruler was also the high priest. In some cases, as with the Pharaohs of Egypt, the Incas of the Peru and the Emperors of ancient China, the ruler claimed to actually be a god or the biological child of a divine being. In this recurring scenario trained priests provided the interpretation of dreams to rulers. Dream messages were often used to reaffirm divinely ordained kingship because they were understood to be direct and compelling communications from the gods.

The Dream Stele of Egyptian Pharaoh Thutmose IV is a clear illustration of Kingship validated by a divinely-inspired dream. Sitting between the giant, stone paws, in front of the great Sphinx in Giza, is a stone pillar on which is inscribed the dream of Thutmose IV. This Dream Stele, also called the *"Sphinx Stele"*, was erected in 1401 BCE the first year of this pharaoh's reign. As was common with other pharaohs, the stele makes claim to divine legitimization for Thutmose IV. It tells the story of the young Prince Thutmose who falls asleep near the Great Sphinx of Giza. At that time the great sphinx was buried up to its chin in the desert sands. While sleeping the young prince dreams that the sphinx, personified as the god Re-Horemakhet, promises him the throne of Egypt in return for Thutmose clearing away the sand which had buried sphinx. Upon waking Thutmose did as he was instructed and undertook the monumental task of clearing the sand from the Sphinx. As the dream had promised, Thutmose IV went on to become the pharaoh. In gratitude, he promoted the god Re-Horemakhet above his father's patron deity Amun-Re, dedicated a temple to Horemakhet, and placed the inscribed stele between the paws of the Sphinx to record the dream story and establish his Kingship.

Despite the priestly focus on politically motivated divination, the healing role of dreams found in the Shamanic traditions, was preserved, in a subsidiary manner, within the context of ancient religions and continued with the classic civilizations. A ready example is seen in ancient Israel where the shamanic role was taken up by the Biblical prophets; holy men who operated independently of the political leaders and the priests. In this context, dreams and visions continued to be understood as an important, communication channel between heaven and earth, and as a source of warning and healing.

Dream healing temples were built throughout the ancient world, dedicated to specific healing deities like the Egyptian god of dreams, Serapis (temple dated to 3000 BCE), or from ancient Greece Hypnos (god of sleep) and Morpheus (god of dreams). These sanctuaries had the explicit purpose of healing through dreams. Pilgrims would flock to visit these curative asylums seeking therapy for physical and emotional disease. With the guidance of well-paid healer/priests, those seeking healing would perform purification rituals which sometimes included the use of narcotics. They would then sleep within the temple in the hope of receiving a healing visitation or message in a dream.

From within the classical, Greek world, the therapeutic cult of Asclepius (Asklepios), a healer- hero turned demiurge, grew popular in the sixth century BCE and continued on for another eight centuries. The central temple dedicated to this supposed divine being, the *"Asclepieion"*, was situated near the city of Epidaurus in southeastern Greece, but there were over 200 other Asclepieions scattered throughout the Greco-Roman world. Seeking cures, using the technique of **dream incubation**, was the main activity at these dream temples. After performing some purification rituals, visitors would sleep over in the temple's special inner sanctum, with the hope of receiving a healing dream. The dream might involve the appearance of Asclepius himself, who could directly heal the dreamer, but more often than not, the dream came in the form of a healing message that would later be interpreted by the priests at the temple. The dream priests would then prescribe the appropriate therapy. The original Hippocratic Oath taken by classical physicians began with the invocation: *"I swear by Apollo the Physician and by Asclepius and by Hygieia and Panacea and by all the gods ..."*

In the context of these ancient, religious/political priesthoods, sophisticated systems of symbols were developed. Some of the earliest written works from the ancient world are lexicons of dream symbols and their interpretations. These include the dream books of the ancient Assyrians and Babylonians recovered from the library of King Ashurbanipal (669-626 BCE) at Nineveh in modern day Iraq, and the Mesopotamian Epic of Gilgamesh which purports to include the first interpreted dream ever recorded in literature. Similar dream lexicons can be found in ancient Egypt, China, Persia and Greece.

The largest, surviving compilation of dream lore, the Oneirocritica (The Meaning of Dreams), was authored, in the second-century, by a professional, Roman, soothsayer, known as Artemidorus of Daldis. The Oneirocritica is a dream dictionary that focuses primarily on deciphering dreams as omens of the future. Dreams are categorized by their symbolic content, and despite its emphasis on divination, this book demonstrates some deep insight into the process of dream symbolization. Artemidorus delineates two broad categories of dreams: ***"insomnium"*** are dreams about mundane, day to day life, while ***"somnium"*** are those that have the prophetic power to reveal the future.

The earliest literary reference to dreams from ancient, classical Greece comes from Homer's Odyssey written in the 8th century BCE. Homer distinguishes between true dreams and false dreams:

"There are two gates through which the dream visions reach us; one is of horn, the other of ivory. Those that come through the ivory gate cheat us with empty promises that never see fulfilment; while those that issue from the gate of burnished horn inform the dreamer what will really happen."

Based on Homer's ideas, the ancient Greeks distinguished between **significant** and **non-significant** dreams. The significant dreams came directly from the gods and pertained to important social and political events, while the insignificant dreams pertained to the less-important, mundane life of the dreamer. This distinction, between two or more different kinds of dreams, is widespread throughout. In various cultures, dreams may be classified as divine or demonic, true or false, important or unimportant, or, as in the Vedic texts of ancient India, lucky or unlucky. The fourth century, Chinese, Taoist sage Lao Tzu (Lieh-Tzü) distinguishes between six types of dreams: *"ordinary dreams, day-residue dreams, dreams of waking, dreams of fear, joyful dreams and terror dreams"*.

Classical philosophers like Socrates (470 – 399 BCE), Plato (427-347 BCE) and especially Aristotle (384-322 BCE), as forerunners of modern science, based their ideas about dreams on reason and logic which must be backed up by empirical evidence. In some of his writings, Plato's attitude towards dreams is quite negative. He viewed most dreams as being false appearances that lead people away from reason and truth, but, although separated by over 2400 years, Plato comes strikingly close to the ideas of Freud when he quotes his teacher Socrates – *"we each possess a lawless, wild beast nature that peers out from sleep"*. Plato goes on to ask, *"How can you prove whether at this moment we are sleeping, and all our thoughts are a dream; or whether we are awake, and talking to one another in the waking state?"* A similar question was asked, about 100 years later, by the famous Chinese philosopher Chuang Tzu (3rd century BCE): Upon awaking from a nap he exclaims, *"I do not know whether I was then a man dreaming I was a butterfly, or whether I am now a butterfly dreaming I am a man."*

It was Plato's student, Aristotle, who fully articulated a major turn in conceptual thinking about dreams. Like a select few of the ancients and most scientific thinkers today, Aristotle viewed dreams as being generated from within the human mind, which he called the soul or psyche (located in the heart rather than the brain), as opposed to encounters with external forces or spirits. For Aristotle, dreams are not encounters with the spirit world or visitations from mysterious, external forces but self-generated events that originate in the psyche of the dreamer. With the Aristotelian shift to thinking of dreams as self-created entities, two trends of thought emerged. One trend was to devalue dreams as meaningless mental images that flicker through the mind and have no real significance. The negative extremity of this train of thought was an abhorrence of dreams as meaningless, deceptive and foolish. The second trend, which emerged from Aristotle's ideas about the psyche, was the recognition of a new focus for dream interpretation: Rather than interpreting dreams as omens of future events, dreams came to be viewed as revelators of the human psyche. A psychological perspective on dreams and the human condition in general began to slowly emerge. For Aristotle the beast was not some external being, but a hidden part of our selves.

In the fourth and fifth centuries BCE, in heyday of classical Greece, Hippocrates (460-377BCE), known as the father of medicine, wrote his <u>Treatise on Dreams</u>, wherein he speaks of dreams as diagnostic tools. His understanding was that dreams reflected the physical condition, which promulgated a method for interpreting dream images in terms of physical disease. For example, he suggests that if one dreams of a rapidly flowing river it indicates issues with the urinary track. Dreams of a house on fire indicate an infection with resultant fever. A fire in the roof of the house indicates the infection is located in the head, or, if in the basement, the infection would be in the bowel, and so on. Hippocrates developed his diagnostic system based on the four humors (bodily fluids) of the body. The four humors of Hippocratic medicine are black bile, yellow bile, phlegm, and blood. Each humor corresponds to one of the main, body organs, and to one of the traditional four temperaments: Sanguine (enthusiastic, active, and social), Choleric (short-tempered, fast-paced, pushy), Melancholic (analytical and quiet), Phlegmatic (relaxed and slow-paced). Hippocrates approach shows an understanding of the link between emotional and physical processes. Good health is achieved when the four humours are in balance. Hippocrates suggested that dreams can reveal an imbalance caused by an overabundance or a paucity of one or more of the humors.

Over five hundred years after Hippocrates, during the height of the Roman Empire, a prominent Greek physician Aelius Galenus (better known as Galen of Pergamon) adopted and refined

Hippocrates's system of medicine and in particular the concept of diagnostic dreams:

> *"The vision-in-sleep (enhypnion), in my opinion, indicates a disposition of the body. Someone dreaming of a conflagration is troubled by yellow bile, but if he dreams of smoke, or mist, or deep darkness, by black bile. Rainstorm indicates that cold moisture abounds; snow, ice, and hail, cold phlegm . . . But since in sleep the soul does not produce impressions based on dispositions of the body only, but also from the things habitually done by us day by day, and some from what we have thought – and indeed some things are revealed by it in fashion of prophesy (for even this is witnessed by experience) – the diagnosis of the body from the visions-in-sleep that arise from the body may become difficult."* (Galeni XIII de Dignotione Ex Insomnus Libellus) 2nd Century C.E.

Although Galen emphasizes the diagnostic aspect of dreaming, it is noteworthy that he also recognizes a psychological and prophetic function of dreams. The idea, that dreams are an early warning of potential disease or injury within the body, is still relevant to dream interpretation today. William Charles Dement (born July 29, 1928) is a pioneering, American sleep-researcher and founder of the Sleep Research Center at Stanford University. He tells a story of being a young research assistant at the University, a time in his life when he was smoking cigarettes heavily. He explains that one morning he woke up feeling very congested and coughing up mucus and bits of pink flesh. He immediately consulted a friend of his who was a medical doctor and was told, to his horror, that in fact he had lung cancer . . . and then he woke up. It was a dream. Dement quit smoking immediately after that, but was convinced that his body was warning him of potential disease and that this dream potentially saved his life.

MEDIEVAL FAIRIES AND FIENDS

Paradoxically, Aristotle's shift, from a divinatory to a psychological perspective, actually reclaimed some of the earlier, Shamanistic notions, which various autocratic priesthoods had down-played. Notwithstanding the priestly focus on divination, and regardless of the philosopher's focus on unyielding reason, dreams persisted to carry import in popular, folk life and lore. Traditional, Shamanistic beliefs and practices continued within the traditions of the common people, especially among marginalized groups living in the shadowy fringes of the priest-king establishments. There were charismatic individuals, outside of the priesthood, who still operated within the mind-set of indigenous folklore. These figures emerge as independent healers, shamans, prophets, soothsayers, sorcerers, witches and wizards – people who have the special gift of being able to communicate with the spirit world through some altered state of consciousness.

Some cultures retained their Shamanic, religious practices throughout the ancient and classical periods and even into modern times. When the Romans occupied the European continent, including the British Isles, during the second century BCE, the indigenous peoples, whom they encountered there, were rooted in an intrinsically, Shamanistic society. With the spread of Christianity and later Islam, many of the pagan, tribal religions were neutralized, but traditional ideas about dreams persisted and often permeated into the folk lore, and even into authorized, religious doctrines of the monotheistic faiths. Similar, shaman-based beliefs and customs were, in fact, infused into the religious canons of all the world's, major religions. We have many prime examples, of dreams providing connections between the world of man and the world of spirit, evident in the Jewish Torah, the Christian Gospels, the Islamic Koran, the Hindu Vedas, the Buddhist Sutras and other sacred texts from around the world.

But, despite the inclusion of some reconfigured, spiritualist beliefs in many, official, religious canons, notions of the demonic quality of dreams were often viewed, fearfully, as a threat to the authority and stability of established political/religious institutions. In light of such conflicts, folkloric, shamanic practices and ideas about dreams were often rigidly suppressed by politically-sponsored priesthoods. This tension, between the indigenous, folk beliefs and the official, state religions, occurred in ancient Egypt, China, India and other antique cultures, but nowhere was it more pronounced than in the medieval, European, Christian Church, where dreams became associated with the Devil and dream-interpretation was viewed as a Satanic practice. Unlike some of the philosophers, who characterized dreams as merely, insignificant superstition, the Christian Church saw most dreams as being the agents of malevolence. The frequent, sexual content of dreams exasperated this attitude in a culture that associated sexual desire with evil and where sexual impulses were severely repressed. Ironically, as Freud pointed out, the more rigorously an individual's sexual impulses are repressed, the more likely it will be that this person will have overtly sexual dreams. Such dreams must have horrified the sensibilities of many medieval Christians. Most often people would be reluctant to recall or share such dreams – the possible consequence of which could be punishment for the practice of sorcery, or condemnation to Hell.

The **succubus** and her male counterpart the **incubus** emerged into the medieval, folk mindset. The succubus is described as a demonic female who has sexual relations with men while they slept, often securing human sperm for the purposes of demonic gestation or to impregnate human women. A succubus often takes the form of a beautiful young girl, but closer scrutiny would reveal irregularities in her body, such as animal claws and teeth or a snake-like tail. Sometimes deformed or autistic children were attributed to unnatural, sexual relations with these demonic seducers. Many, including King James I, also correlated the succubae to nocturnal emissions. Such ideas were not merely the superstitions of uneducated folk, but, as we have seen, found their way into the written doctrines of the Christian Church. These beliefs obviously revert back, from the philosophic view of dreams as self generated phenomenon, to the earlier, exoteric concepts of dreams resulting from the intrusion of outside forces, or activity in an external, dream dimension.

THE IMAGINATIVE FACULTY AND PERCEPTION

During ancient and medieval times, in India and China, philosophers, scholars and priests were also researching and theorizing about dreams. The Vedas (ancient Sanskrit literature from the Indian subcontinent) developed sophisticated ideas about the nature and meaning of dreams that, in many ways, surpassed those of the Classical Greek and Roman writers. They frequently anticipate modern, scientific concepts, especially on the matter of **sensory perception**. In the Hindu Vedas and many of the Chinese, Buddhist writings it was postulated that sensory experience of the world is, primarily, a mental reconstruction of energies from within the human psyche. This implies that the material world is actually a hallucinatory illusion.

This same idea surfaced in the writings of subsequent, medieval, European thinkers like Maimonides and Thomas Aquinas. They developed the concept of a human ***"imaginative faculty"***, and probed ideas about the relationship between conscious experience and perception. Modern scientists have also come to understand that our experience, of the world, is a construct of our minds, occurring as much in our brain as in our sensory organs. A simplified example: When we see the colour red, a specific frequency of electromagnetic radiation interacts on receptors within the eye. This wave pattern is then communicated to the brain which constructs the colour red as we experience it. We have no way of knowing if one person's experience is the same as another's. Our entire, sensory perception happens in this way – the brain reconstructing energy waves into images, sounds, tastes, smells and tactile sensations. The same faculty that facilitates sensory perception is also at play with our dreams except that, instead of reconstructing sensory information from the physical world, it constructs imagery and other sensations from a deep reserve of unconscious memories.

⁂ ⁂ ⁂ ⁂ ⁂ ⁂ ⁂ ⁂

CHAPTER THREE
THE SCIENCE OF SLEEP AND DREAMING

Before we go on to interpret and analyze dreams, it is helpful to reinforce our understanding of dreaming with some quantifiable, physiological research. With technological advances in brain study, a lot of clinical laboratory work has been done on sleep and dreams. In the 1950's and 60's clinical psychology found itself theoretically at odds with psychoanalysis and other depth psychologies. But, significantly, many of the clinical studies have actually reinforced some ideas hypothesized by depth psychologists.

As early as the eighteen hundreds, Scientists had discovered that the human body carried electrical signals throughout – the heart, brain and nerves being the most electrically active parts of the body. The Electrocardiograph machine, which measured electrical activity in the heart, was developed in 1902. Medical scientists applied this technology to observing the brain. In 1929, a German psychiatrist, Hans Berger developed a mechanism that detected and recorded brain waves – the, now familiar, **EEG** or **Electroencephalogram**. Berger used electrodes, taped to a subject's skull, as a harmless, non-invasive technique for recording brain function. The taped-on electrodes were connected to an electronic, recording device, allowing scientists to measure and record electrical activity in the brain. The readout was a wave pattern that was originally printed out on a long roll of paper – today the wave patterns can be seen on a computer monitor.

Subsequent digital technology has opened the door for increasingly more detailed mapping of the human brain. The EEG is used to research and diagnose a variety of disorders including neurological and psychiatric. Much research has also been dedicated to measuring the EEG patterns of sleeping and dreaming subjects under diverse, controlled conditions.

IDENTIFIYING THE DREAMING BRAIN

A major breakthrough, in sleep/dream research, occurred in 1953 at the University of Chicago. Two scientists Eugene Aserinsky and Nathaniel Kleitman conducted experiments by monitoring the electrical signals from the brains of sleeping subjects. The EEG (electroencephalogram) was used to monitor brain waves –but soon Aserinsky and Kleitman were able to monitor other aspects of the sleeping body by attaching electrodes. The Electromyogram (EMG) measures muscle tone in the neck and shoulders of the sleeping subject, and the Electrooculogram (EOG) which measures the eye-movements of the sleeper. Their research led to some fascinating discoveries. They observed a regular pattern or cycle of sleep which they defined in five main stages (some subsequent researchers redefined the sleep cycle with only four stages). As a subject fell asleep their regular high frequency brain waves would gradually become slower, larger and less regular, progressively bringing the person into deep sleep. The process would then cycle around and back with brain waves gradually increasing in frequency and regularity as the subject returned back towards waking consciousness. But something unexpected happens just before the cycle should end with waking up. Instead of waking-up, the sleeping subject enters a special state of sleep, which early researchers called **REM (Rapid Eye Movement).** REM is marked with several distinct characteristics. The feature, which gives REM its name, is the continuous rapid movements of the eyes beneath the closed lids – acting as if they are, in effect, seeing as they do in waking life. In the REM stage of sleep, brain-wave activity is similar to waking patterns. During the REM sleep state, there is also a complete paralysis of most of the muscles in the body. A person's body, in REM sleep, goes completely limp. This may account for the common experience of paralysis of limbs and voice, often experienced by dreamers while dreaming or right upon waking. In addition, REM sleep is characterized by sexual arousal in both men and women. Heartbeat and breathing also become irregular. Within the sleep cycle, the REM stage will last for a varying period of time, usually from fifteen to thirty-five minutes, before returning back into the deep, slow-wave, non-REM stages of sleep, or to awakening.

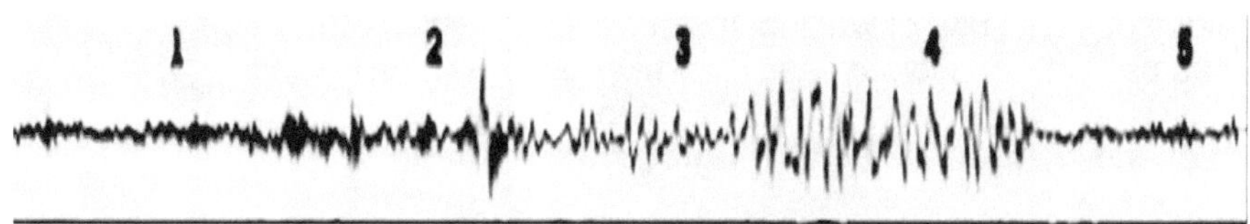

ONE AVERAGE ADULT SLEEP/DREAM CYCLE : 90-120 minutes

Non-REM Sleep				REM Sleep
Stage 1 Approx. 4 - 5% total cycle time	**Stage 2** Approx 45 - 55% total cycle time	**Stage 3** Approx 4 - 6 % total cycle time	**Stage 4** Approx 12 - 15% total cycle time	**Stage 5** Approx 20-25% total cycle time
Alpha Waves	Beta Waves	Delta Waves	Delta Waves	Theta Waves
Light sleep	Falling Unconscious	Deep sleep Starts	Very Deep sleep	REM
Brain activity decreases by 50%	Brain waves slow down - occasional small bursts of brain activity.	Brain begins to produce slow delta waves	Brain produces only delta waves	Brain waves speed up - activity similar to waking state
Eye movement and muscle activity slow Subject may experience muscle twitches	Eye and muscle movements sparse, intermittent. Some tossing and turning may occur. Teeth grinding may occur.	There is very little or no eye or muscle movement	No muscle or eye movement Slow Rhythmic Breathing Body temperature decreases. Blood pressure decreases.	Muscles paralyzed. Eye movement quick, and irregular. Heart/breathing rates increase Blood pressure rises. Penile erections or vaginal moistening and clitoral stimulation
Subject can be easily aroused.	Loss of waking consciousness	Sleepers awakened will feel groggy. .	Difficult to awaken Rare dreams abstract.	Frequent vivid, sequential, dreaming

The Sleep Cycle moves from Stage I through 2, 3, and 4 to REM, then around again through stages 2, 3, 4 and back to REM, repeatedly, throughout the sleep period. Each cycle normally lasts from 90 to 110 minutes. Sleepers will usually experience four to five REM phases in a seven hour sleep. Periods of REM tend to get longer, with each subsequent cycle, as the sleep period progresses. Towards the end of sleeping, the individual does not recycle from REM into stages 2, 3 or 4 as the body prepares to wake up. Most often a sleeper wakes up directly from REM.

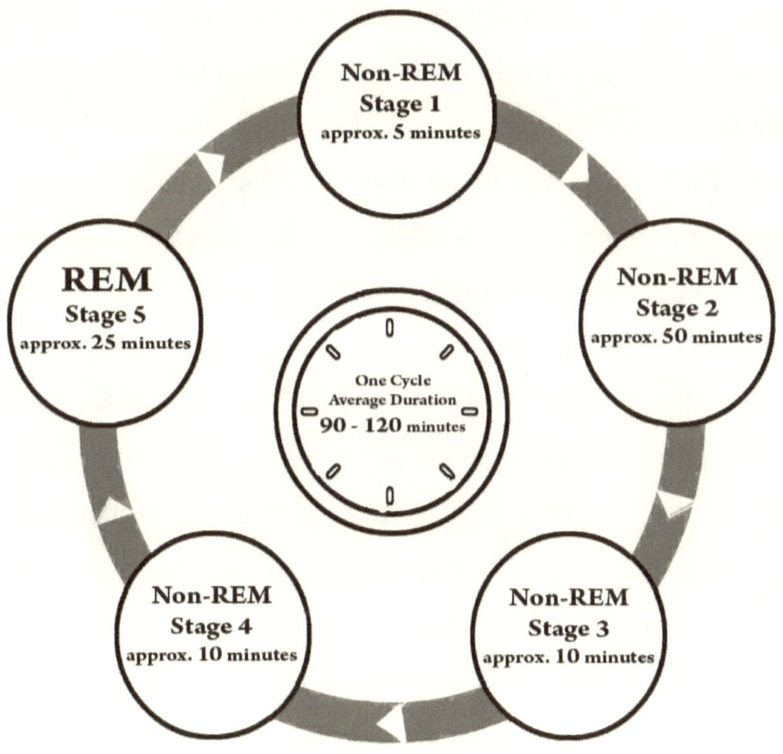

A fascinating aspect of the normal REM phase, of the sleep cycle, is the mechanism whereby, during the most dynamic period of neural activity, the body's voluntary, motor functions are completely paralyzed. This loss of muscle tone and control during REM is referred to as **REMatonia**. REMatonia acts as a safety mechanism, preventing dreamers from physically acting out their dreams. Despite extensive studies, researchers have not been able to track exactly how this mechanism works. It has been hypothesized that the trigger is located in the **medulla oblongata** (or medulla), a conical, stem-like structure located in the brainstem. The medulla connects the higher functions of the brain to the spinal cord and controls the interface between the brain and most muscular functions. As a sleeping person enters the REM stage, autonomic functions, like breathing, heartbeat and digestion remain active. Some autonomic functions also remain interactive. For example, if one is having an erotic dream, heartbeat and breathing may react as if one were actually engaged in sexual activity. Although most muscles are immobilized in REM, the eyes, of course, continue to move about and sexual arousal still occurs.

The sleep cycle is subject to a number of irregularities that directly affect dreaming. The pattern changes with age and fluctuates with medical conditions, emotional state, drug use and sleep deprivation. Clinical research shows that newborns experience REM for approximately 75% of their sleep time. At one year a child will spend approximately 66% of sleep time in REM, and this diminishes down to 20% of sleep time in adults.

Work schedules and alarm clocks may also impose atypical shifts in our normal sleep cycle.

LIFE WITHOUT REM

The discovery and study of the sleep cycle has gone a long way towards discerning a general, physiological pattern for dreaming. We've come to understand the two basic sleep states: **NREM** which is characterized by no rapid eye movements and **REM** which is characterized by a lot of rapid eye movements. Numerous studies have shown that the vast majority of recalled dreams occurred in the REM state, and very few in NREM. In the early clinical studies, when test subjects were roused from the non-REM stages of sleep, they rarely reported that they were dreaming. When a sleeping subject was awakened from REM sleep, they almost always reported that they were dreaming and, often, dreaming vividly. By identifying the REM phase of the sleep cycle, researchers were able to determine, with quite accurate precision, when a subject was dreaming.

Identifying the sleep cycle, which we all experience each night, and particularly **REM sleep = dreaming**, led to a series of interesting findings. Arising from repeated clinical studies, one poignant discovery was that: when monitored subjects were deprived of REM sleep – that is they are awoken whenever they entered REM, they would, within a couple of days, begin to show various signs of psychotic behaviour even when allowed NREM sleep. The sleep cycle, of the REM-deprived subjects, also changed radically. After 36 -48 hours of REM deprivation, subjects would skip the initial, NREM stages of sleep and enter immediately into REM. If further sleep-deprived, subjects would begin to hallucinate. In other words, they would begin to dream while still awake. The findings of sleep-deprivation studies provide strong indicators about the function of dreams. Since REM sleep deprivation leads to psychotic behaviour, it follows that dreaming, itself, must be an essential process to maintain a functionally balanced psyche.

BEYOND REM

The idea, that REM sleep indicates dreaming, became the paradigm that sleep researchers based their work on, for several decades, until the end of the 20th century. But more recent studies have shown, unexpectedly, that we do also dream, albeit infrequently, in **NREM** (non-REM) stages of sleep. Unlike REM dreams which occur invariably throughout the REM sleep stage, dreams in NREM stages of sleep are much less frequent and do not occur with any predictable regularity. So far, sleep-scientists have not been able to determine a regular pattern for Delta (NREM) dreams, nor have they tracked any physiological markers, which would distinguish dreaming from non-dreaming, within the Delta brain-wave states. My own eclectic research suggests something of the nature of these deep-sleep dreams. NREM dreams have a different quality about them when compared to REM dreams. NREM dreams are generally brief and rarely have a story-line, while REM dreams often follow a narrative, although the chain of events often seems bizarre and apparently irrational. REM is also the arena for erotic dreams, which often prove to be highly pleasurable, and sometimes inappropriate to our waking sensibilities.

While REM dreams can be very positive and enjoyable, REM is also the stage for disturbing dreams and nightmares. REM dreams are often emotionally charged – sometimes with conflicting or negative emotions. On the other hand, subjects report that most NREM dreams are fragments of detached thinking or sensory or emotional experiences. I have also had reports of, what might be called, spiritual and other-worldly experiences during NREM sleep.

CHAPTER FOUR
UNCOVERING THE UNCONSCIOUS, MODERN DEPTH PSYCHOLOGIES

At the dawn of the 20th century, many conventional scientists identified dreams as meaningless epiphenomenon of sleep, or stray energy emissions that occur randomly within our brains. These cerebral emissions were generally viewed as psychic residue devoid of meaning for good or bad. Believing that dreams were significant was usually viewed as foolhardy, superstitious nonsense. But this was to forever change with the publication in 1899 of <u>The Interpretation of Dreams</u> by Sigmund Freud. With his ground-breaking work, Sigmund Freud opened the door to the scientific study of dreams, laying the foundation for a new scientific discipline, **Psychoanalysis.** A whole, new field, of related research and therapeutic approaches, often referred to as **Psychodynamic or Depth Psychologies,** opened up. Ironically some primordial Shamanistic concepts re-emerged, although somewhat transformed, within the context of modern, psychoanalytic theory.

Freud coined many terms that have become familiar, in modern parlance – **unconscious mind, id, ego, libido, repression, suppression, projection, neurosis, pleasure-principle, Freudian slip, taboo** and many more. At the base of his work Freud provided a new model, which identified components that make up the human psyche: the **id,** the **ego** and the **super-ego**. These components may be compared to the physical systems in the human body, working together, each with its specific function. The Id is Freud's term for the animal component of the human psyche which seeks self-gratification, pleasure and fulfillment of its wishes and desires, including sexuality, self-propagation and continued existence. Opposite and often in conflict with the Id is the Superego. The Superego represents the moral aspect of the psyche which determines social and ethical inclination, often as a check-balance for the potentially dangerous drives of the Id. In-between the Id and the Superego is the Ego, which represents an individual's sense of self.

Although he was the first to establish this scientific model, Freud's tri-part, psychoanalytic view, of the human psyche, is really

not a new one, being preconceived within the Judeo/Christian idea of a good inclination(Superego) and an evil(Id) inclination, which influence the individual (Ego). In fact, the individual's struggle with conflicting good and evil impulses is endemic to most religious systems. The idea is also entrenched in popular wisdom, throughout the ages, as witnessed by countless cartoons depicting the image of a person (ego) with an angel (super-ego) on one shoulder, and a demon (id) on the other.

Freud also defined three states of consciousness, used by most Depth Psychologists today, as the context within which the various elements of the psyche operate: **i) Consciousness** – this includes all external and internal stimuli and information which we are conscious of.

ii) Preconscious – This includes the stimuli and information that we have stored, readily available just below the surface of our consciousness. For example: If someone asks you when your birthday is, although this information is not in your immediate consciousness, you will be able easily and quickly reach into the top drawer of your memory storeroom, and retrieve the information.Also included in the pre-conscious category are immediate stimuli that we are unaware of because we are focused elsewhere. For example: As I sit here writing on my computer, an electrical fan is whirring over my head, but most of the time I am unaware of the sound. If I stop and listen I will immediately become conscious of the sound.

iii) **Unconscious** – The idea, that there is a whole lot of essential, psychological processing going on below the surface of our consciousness is central to most mystic traditions, but it was Freud who first put forward a scientific theory of the unconscious. In fact, the concept of an **active unconscious** is the foundation stone of psychoanalytic theory. Although we are usually not directly aware of its workings our unconscious functions to maintain our psyche, just as our autonomic physical processes like breathing or blood circulation, operate unconsciously to sustain our physical bodies. Psychoanalysis is based on the understanding that our behavior in waking life is profoundly influenced by motivations from our unconscious. *(Note: The term **unconscious,** in lay parlance, is sometimes interchanged with **subconscious**.)

One of the main functions of dreams, in Freud's view, is ***"wish fulfillment",*** to ameliorate or satisfy the primitive desires of our animal nature. But the idea of wish fulfillment goes, beyond our animal nature, into the egotistical complexities of human emotion, psychological patterns, and self-image.

Freud's pioneering approach to dream interpretation is based on the idea that dreams are composed of symbols that disguise their real meanings. The disguise allows the dreamer to satisfy unconscious desires, free from the self-conscious, superego inhibitors of waking consciousness. For Freud, understanding a dream usually involves deciphering the secret code unique to each individual dreamer. This is done with a process of ***"free association"*** which leads inward, from the superficial, dream symbol, or ***"manifest content"*** of the dream, towards the actual, operative but hidden meaning or ***"latent content"*** of the dream. With free association the basic technique is to associate instantly whatever pops into one's mind without imposing any form of conscious control or censorship over the association.

Although working from the conceptual ground that Freud had paved, Carl Jung, Freud's early protégé and later rival, took a different approach to interpreting dream symbols. Jung identified a process of human, psychological development that he termed *"the process of individuation"*. The unconscious was the realm of, not just the animal nature within man, but also the source of a sublime nature that worked to guide an individual on their spiritual journey through life. In Jung's view, instead of concealing unconscious desires, the purpose of the dream is to communicate something from the unconscious to the conscious mind. For Jung, the dream symbol is not a disguise, but a direct representation of a primal, psychological idea, usually conveyed in a pre-verbal language. Jung also put forward the idea of *"archetypical"* dream symbols – symbols generated, not only by the work of the individual dreamer's psyche, but symbols that are built into the human psyche and shared, by all humans in, what he termed *"the collective unconscious"*. Unlike the Freudian approach, rather than leading the dreamer away from the symbol towards the latent or actual meaning by free association, Jung's method of dream interpretation is to stay focused on the dream content itself, using *"direct association"* to derive meaning from the symbols. With direct association the method is not the immediate uncensored response as with free association, but a process where the dreamer considers what the symbol means to themselves and in the context of the archetypical meanings of a particular symbol.

In my own work with dreams, I have found that both methods, Freud's Free Association and Jung's Direct Association, are useful and valid approaches towards a comprehensive understanding of a dream's symbolism.   To the point, Freud's and Jung's approaches are not mutually exclusive. Using both concurrently, as we will do in Part II of this book, offers the most meaningful elucidations of most dreams.

REPRESSION, THE DARK SIDE AND THE FUNCTION OF DREAMS

The concept of repression is pertinent to Freudian, Jungian and most other, current, psycho-dynamic approaches to dream interpretation. Consider the following paradigm:

A wild, young horse is penned up in a small space, unable to run, without respite. Three things will happen:

i)   At first the horse will become restless, agitated and angry, pacing and kicking.

ii)   After a long while the horse will become docile and spiritless, barely conscious.

iii)   After an even longer while, unable to run, the horse will become physically weak, its muscles atrophied and rigid.

If, at last, this unfortunate horse is finally released, out onto the open pasture, it will be, both physically and mentally, unable to run free and to pursue its natural destiny. Nor would one be able to ride on such a beast. Only in rare cases, with intense rehabilitation and exercise, would such a horse be able to re-approach fulfillment of its natural potential.

We have seen that, in the Freudian view, there are three essential components of the human personality. These are the **Id**, the **Ego** and the **Superego**. The Id encompasses the primitive, animal core aspect of the self and includes our most basic, physical needs and desires. Often our animal urges, including sexuality and aggression, must be repressed in order for us to function within society and in relation to the other elements of our psyche. The animal-self (Id) often encounters conflicts with the dictates and expectations of society and with an individual's sense of morality (superego), and with personal self-image (ego). Much of this conflict is unconscious and will frequently be expressed in dreams. This suggests one of the main functions of dreams – **in the open field of our unconscious, our wild self can run free** – we can express all the aspects of ourselves including our animal nature, which (id) is a vital aspect of our, whole, human being. We function better holistically, as human beings, when the animal element of ourselves is also active and functional. Without our dreams, to allow our inner beast out of its cage on a regular basis, this vital aspect of ourselves would never develop its full potential. Overly-repressed, frustrated energies may leak out of the unconscious, and into the pre-conscious and conscious life, in the form of negative or destructive thoughts, emotions and behaviour. Just like the horse, unable to run, we may experience anger, frustration, and then apathy and depression; what Freud termed ***"neurosis"*** and eventually a dysfunctional psyche, ***"psychosis"***. Freud himself used the analogy of a horse and rider in describing the relationship of Id and the Ego.

> *"The functional importance of the ego is manifested in the fact that normally control over the approaches to motility devolves upon it. Thus in its relation to the id it is like a man on horseback, who has to hold in check the superior strength of the horse; with this difference, that the rider tries to do so with his own strength while the ego uses borrowed forces. The analogy may be carried a little further. Often a rider, if he is not to be parted from his horse, is obliged to guide it where it wants to go; so in the same way the ego is in the habit of transforming the id's will into action as if it were its own."* <u>(Complete Works of Sigmund Freud</u>. (1923-26) <u>The Ego and the Id</u> .)

But Freudian psychoanalysis was neither the only nor the first tradition to recognize repression as a force in the human psyche. Originating from early medieval China, there is a charming series of Ch'an (Zen in Japan) Buddhist, illustrated poems, The Ox-Herding Poems, which uses a similar metaphor to describe the natural process of attaining our innate, human potential. There are many, illustrated versions of these poems, describing in stages, the process of finding, capturing, taming, and riding a wild Ox. The Ox-Herding Poems provide an excellent paradigm for the interaction between our higher, human nature and our animal nature. Each stage in the process appears on a separate page and is illustrated by a drawing. The Ox represents our animal self. The Ox-Rider represents our higher, conscious self. With dreamlike imagery, rendered in ink on rice-paper, the ox-herding series describes the process of discovering and finally working in perfect harmony with our animal nature. This paradigm culminates with the ox (body/animal self) and the rider (conscious self) operating effortlessly as one entity on a journey home. The ox-herding exemplar is not unlike many other mystic traditions that seek to harmonize our physical and spiritual realities. The idea is, not to annihilate or sublimate our animal selves, but to integrate our physical nature with our human/spiritual nature. In the final panels, Ox and Rider are thoroughly attuned so that the Rider travels effortlessly without any endeavour at control. The fully trained Ox unquestioningly does the will of its master, while the rider completely trusts the Ox to take him safely home.

In many respects, psychoanalytic concepts are re-embodiments of mystic, religious traditions and especially Eastern mysticism. In mystic traditions, as in psychoanalytic theory, dreams, visions and altered states of consciousness are the connecting factors – the bridges between worlds. Carl Jung, who was profoundly influenced by concepts of Taoism and other Eastern spiritual traditions, restated, somewhat, the message found in the Ox Herding series. As we have seen, he identified a spiritual journey called the ***"individuation process,"*** whereby one could come to know, what Jung called the *"shadow self,"* referring to the dark, hidden aspect of each person's psyche. As a person matures psychologically the shadow self gradually emerges and is absorbed into the whole personality. The shadow self appears to us in many guises in dreams. From a Jungian perspective, the union of the shadow self into the whole personality is a central feature of the self-actualization or individuation process. With individuation Jung introduced the idea that there was is a universal, transformative process; a journey towards realizing our full human potential.

Jung also spoke about the ***"anima"*** and ***"animus"***, the female aspect within each male, and the male aspect within each female. Like the shadow self, the anima/animus, is revealed and integrated into the whole person, through the individuation process. Jung's ideas diverged from Freud's, approach, which was geared towards healing psychological disease and disorders. While Jung emphasized the collective unconscious and universal archetypical symbols, Freud focussed on the individual unconscious and healing psychological disorders. According to both Freud and Jung, there are aspects of our psyches that our conscious ego does not want to see. By and large, these facets of ourselves remain concealed and harmless, in the shadows, within our unconscious. But, when these hidden, character complexes impinge upon and interfere with one's functional, conscious life, they generate emotional conflict, which we must then uncover in order to heal ourselves. To bring our shadow self into the light might be painful, but, once exposed, the negativity can be diffused. The more open one is to recognizing the shadow self, the more self-control one gains. We may even discover positive aspects of ourselves that had long been hidden away. Self knowledge is key to self-empowerment and healing. However the human beast, within each individual, is a very personal beast and ultimately remains concealed.

Both, Freudian, psychological healing and Jung's, individuation process imply a progression of human transformation that features a gradual assimilation of unconscious elements of one's psyche with the conscious. Gradually the beast is tamed, conflicts are resolved and hidden barriers are revealed. Ideally, a person achieves

integration so harmonious that one could safely ride the proverbial
bull through a china shop. We are at one with our **humanimal**.

CHAPTER FIVE
THE POWER AND POETRY OF DREAM SYMBOLS

A dream is like a multi-faceted jewel, bringing a range of ideas, emotions and sensations into a unified whole. The nature of most dreams is symbolic, expressed in an exquisitely versatile language, full of nuance that only the dreamer truly understands. It is the language that we use to communicate with ourselves. Understanding the nature of your personal, symbolic vocabulary is the key to interpreting your dreams.

The generation of meaningful symbols is a primary function of the human psyche. Symbols may be the creations of our individual psyches, as per Freud, or they may be archetypes, which are inherited symbols that are embedded in, what Jung called, the *"collective unconscious"*. In both instances, we need to recognize that symbols are more than visual representations of ideas or emotions. Symbols have power and reality unto themselves. The most powerful, dream symbols have multiple aspects, of both personal elements (associations specific to an individual), and archetypical (endemic to the psyches of most humans).

Archetypical symbols tend to repeatedly emerge in world mythologies, as well as in dreams. Take for example the archetypical symbol of Water. Water, as a basic element, represents several very potent, universal concepts. Water often connects with the realm of emotions. If we dream of swimming, bathing or being immersed in water, we are likely moving into the deep, fluid realms of emotion. Water is also associated with the essential life-giving force, nurturing and refreshing. It is universally recognized as a primary source of purification, and has strong associations with birth and rebirth. Many dreamers have reported experiencing profound dream-memories of pre-natal experiences, floating in the watery world of our amniotic sacks. A body of water, an ocean, a lake, even a deep well, may represent the unconscious itself. There are also negative and destructive forces, such as drowning or flooding, which are symbolically associated with water. When we dream of an elemental icon like water, the image may hit us with the force of all our senses; we may see, smell, taste, touch and hear a symbol, while, at the same time, being impacted with the emotional force of the all the ideas and feelings it carries.

All of the above associations to water, positive and negative, are archetypical in nature – they derive from inherent memories and have the same general connotations for human beings across the spectrum of various, cultural contexts. But there are also more specific associations that refine the meaning and power of a symbol. These private symbols derive from two categories: **culturally-specific associations** and **individually-specific associations**, both based on memory of past events.

The trappings of a particular culture will certainly colour one's dreams. The significance of animal symbols is a clear example of this. In western European and American culture the bat is usually considered an ominous and evil creature of darkness, while in Chinese tradition the bat is viewed as a symbol of happiness and joy; The dung beetle, which in most modern circles is considered a rather distasteful insect, was considered a symbol of eternal rebirth by the ancient Egyptians; The Raven appears as a playful trickster in the legends of West Coast, North American, indigenous peoples, but is viewed as an ominous harbinger of death in western European folklore. There are countless more examples where a particular symbol, like an animal or a natural element, has different connotations specifically significant to a particular milieu. Cultural and religious imagery is naturally infused into dream symbols. A Buddhist monk living in Thailand will likely dream of images derived from Buddhist art and mythology, while a Christian living in Rome will more probably dream of biblical images. One might find themselves in a magnificent temple pagoda, the other in a lofty cathedral. Both might dream of angels and demons (surprisingly similar in both traditions). Specific symbolic meanings will also develop among smaller collectives, like families and other social groups.

Of course a single, dream symbol usually incorporates combined archetypical and personal imagery. The meanings of dream symbols become even more profound and multi-layered when archetypical associations are augmented in the particular, dream dialect of an individual. This means that, in addition to culturally engendered symbols each individual has their own personal, symbolic language culled from a lifetime of memories. Many of these memories are stored in our unconscious until they reemerge in a passing recollection or a dream. Persons, places, things, colours, sounds and smells carry associations based on past experience. These numerous, memory-based associations are subtly woven, by the psyche, into symbolic imagery charged with meaning – significant only to the individual. For example: When I was a child I experienced the traumatic experience of falling into a freezing creek when the ice I was standing on cracked beneath my feet. Luckily my father, who had warned me to stay off the ice, was nearby and, grabbing my arm, pulled me out of the icy water almost immediately. Since then the memory of the piercing cold water and my fortunate rescue has taken on symbolic significance for me. If I dream about that frozen creek, which I have on several occasions, it will usually signify imminent danger due to my own carelessness, and sometimes it will signify a narrow escape. By association, when I dream of a frozen creek I may also be connecting to my relationship with my father and the personality traits he represents. My personal associations reverberate powerfully for me but, probably would not resonate with most other people.

HOW DOES AN ENTITY BECOME A SYMBOL?

How does it happen that an object or action comes to represent another object, action or idea? The generation of dream symbols is a complex and intricate process. In his renowned work, <u>The Interpretation of Dreams</u>, Freud outlined a list of associative connections, upon which symbols are constructed, according to the principle of the *"association by resemblance."*
Some of the ways in which association by resemblance works are as follows:

- Association by resemblance in shape.
- Association by resemblance in function.
- Association by resemblance in action.
- Association by resemblance in color.
- Association by resemblance in value.
- Association by resemblance in number.
- Association by resemblance in sound.
- Association by resemblance in quality.
- Association by resemblance in personal quality.
- Association by resemblance in physical position.
- Association by resemblance in status.

In addition to association by resemblance, there are other ways in which items may come to signify other items or ideas. There is an old, folk maxim that *"dreams are contraries"*, suggesting that the core-meaning (latent content) of a dream is essentially the opposite of the explicit meaning (manifest content). This is especially relevant to one of Freud's hypothesises regarding the symbolic, associative process. Freud wrote that: *"inversion or transformation into the opposite is one of the most favoured and most versatile methods of representation which the dreamwork has at its disposal"*. (Freud, Interpretation of Dreams, 1900)

In other words, sometimes the image we recognize in a dream is the diametric opposite of the idea it represents. One of my clients had dreams with the recurring image of a shabby, rundown house, which belonged to him. After deep analysis, which included both free and direct associations, we found that the shabby hut actually symbolized a magnificent palace. Every detail in the hovel was a parallel inversion of a wished-for detail in the palace. The small size of the hovel represented the grand size of the palace; a dusty, threadbare, green rug symbolized a plush, red carpet; tarnished, tin door-knobs stood for gleaming, gold ones; a bare, grimy light-bulb represented a splendid, crystal chandelier. My client had dreamt of his magnificent palace in contrary terms. Every aspect of this imagery represented an inversion of what it actually represented.

Of course the analysis went further because, while the dilapidated cottage represented the palace, the palace embodied aspects of the dreamer's personality. His dreaming mind portrayed his aspirations (the magnificent palace) together with his fear of loss (the shabby hovel).The essential meaning of the dream was about my client's aspirations and fear of losing certain aspects of his personality.

The idea of contrary meanings can be confusing, but think about the use of sarcasm in common speech. One might say, *"he's a really nice guy"*, when what one actually means is *"he's not a very nice person"*. Depending on vocal intonation and the facial expression of the speaker, we know exactly what is being communicated, though the words state the opposite. One could say that the dreaming mind is capable of sarcasm, but it might be tricky to recognize it.

Freud is also famously quoted as saying *"Sometimes a cigar is just a cigar,"* indicating that we must also allow for the possibility that an object or action in a dream simply represents itself. So how is one to accurately interpret a dream symbol, given all the possible, formative associations that may generate them? In order to understand the language of the unconscious mind, one must somehow connect with it. This is where the analytic process begins. As we shall see in Part II, the starting point is **free association** because, with free association, we seek to make unadulterated connections directly to the unconscious.

THE POETRY OF DREAMS

> *"The poet's eye, in a fine frenzy rolling, doth glance from heaven to Earth, from Earth to heaven; and as imagination bodies forth the forms of things unknown, the poet's pen turns them to shape, and gives to airy nothing a local habitation and a name; such tricks hath strong imagination.*" **William Shakespeare, Midsummer Night's Dream.**

A fascinating feature of dream symbols is the artistry with which our unconscious, imaginative faculty combines imagery to create subtle nuances of meaning. For example, if one were to dream of a river, every recalled feature, of that river, will inform our interpretation. Was the river wide or narrow? Were the waters fast moving or slow? Was the water clear or muddied, warm or cold, etc. etc.? Every detail will afford a shade of meaning onto the core symbol, communicating to the dreamer highly complex and multi-layered ideas in a unified, precise and concise form. No wonder poets are often called dreamers.

CAMOUFLAGE OR COSTUME, DRESSING OR DISGUISE?

Freud attributed the artful cloaking, of imagery in dreams, to the ego's propensity for disguising elements. Why the disguise? According to Freud, there may be certain aspects of the unconscious that are unacceptable to the dreamer's waking-ego or self-image. In order for the dream to proceed past the ego's censorship, the unconscious covers up the objectionable material with a clever camouflage. In my own dream work, I have often found the **Clever Disguise Model** to be valuable in terms of getting to the core meanings of many dreams. In the context of dream therapy, this manifests itself in the phenomenon of **resistance,** whereby a dreamer will, initially and very actively, object to an interpretation which latter turns out to be valid. As Shakespeare wrote *"methinks the Lady doth protest too much"*. So too, in the dream therapy process, when a dreamer seems disturbed by or overly dismissive of a certain interpretation, it often points to the validity of that very interpretation. Every dream is an unfolding mystery that only the dreamer can fully understand but, often, it is a challenging process. Resistance poses one of the biggest challenges to interpreting one's own dreams. When it comes to recognizing and overcoming resistance, the support of a dream therapist may be very helpful (more on this later).

However the imaginative power of a symbol is much more than a disguise. We must take our understanding beyond the concept of ego-censorship or filtering x-rated unconscious material. A King or Queen wearing a bejewelled crown does so, not so much to cover their head, but to reveal royal splendour.

Among many traditional cultures masks are used in the ritual re-enactments of mythology. The mask, at once, provides anonymity to the wearer, while revealing an inner, mythological character or idea. Just so, a dream symbol conveys an idea. **Like a mask, a dream symbol can, at once, hide and reveal.** A character, appearing in a dream, is most often, **not a specific person but a multifaceted symbol**. Very often, the idea being conveyed is so intricate and multi-layered that it defies verbal description. But verbiage in dreams may also be charged with symbolic power. In my research and therapy sessions, I have often been awed by the shear, poetic brilliance of the dreaming mind. A single, artfully-constructed, dream symbol may instantly convey a multiplex of meaning that might require many written pages to explain.

FUNNY WORDS, PUNS AND IDIOMS

When interpreting dreams, look for lots of verbal puns and double-entendres – experience has shown me that dreams are loaded with these. Turns and twists of verbal language, such as double entendre, irony, sarcasm, alliteration and even rhyme, often provide clues to interpreting dream symbols. This is a surprisingly common feature that I have observed in my own dream research.

Freud noted that these linguistic camouflages are powerful, literary tools used by creative writers. Strange turns of speech are also commonly used in the telling of jokes (often of an off-colour nature). Sometimes the strange word plays found in dreams make me laugh. I personally recall a funny dream, where it was literally raining dogs and cats. Indubitably, the unconscious is often very funny and, in fact, our sense of humour is seated in the unconscious. I have worked with dreams that turn out to be comparable to a bawdy joke that the dreamer is telling themselves, but the joke also usually carries a candid message.

This type of symbolic wordplay is very frequent in the language of dreams. Decoding visual images based on language can be quite entertaining but avoid overlooking the obvious. Several years I go I helped one of my students with the interpretation of a dream. She began retelling the dream as follows: *"I was riding a white donkey backwards down a path . . ."* The dream went on with other details. I was immediately struck with the visual image of riding a donkey backwards – it was simply a visual representation of a common, slang idiom in English – to do something **"ass-backwards"**. When I pointed this out to the dreamer, she was surprised and had completely overlooked this obvious significance. Her dream had produced a visual representation of a slang idiom that stated its meaning very clearly, and yet, she had entirely failed to notice this glaring interpretation. After working with this dream for some time, it turned out that the dream message was, in fact, warning the dreamer to avoid going down a specific life path *"ass-backwards"*. The symbol, of riding a *white donkey*, also had additional, religious significance for this dreamer.

Another common form of dream wordplay is **alliteration**: a dream symbol may represent something else that has a similar sound, but totally different meaning. An excellent example of this comes from the Biblical book of Jeremiah, Chapter One, Verse 11. The prophet is experiencing a vision, which comes to him in symbolic form. The visions are accompanied by a heavenly voice that guides him with the interpretation of the symbols.

"Moreover the word of the Lord came unto me, saying: 'Jeremiah what seest thou? And I said: 'I see a branch of an almond tree.' Then said the angel of the Lord unto me: 'Thou has seen well for I watch over My word to perform it."

In the above quote the prophet is shown the branch of an Almond tree which he is told represents God's watchfulness. How is the connection made? The words for **almond-tree (*shaked*)** and **watchfulness** *(shoked)* sound very similar, in the original, Biblical Hebrew. One comes to represent the other; by association of similar sound, the almond tree represents God's watchfulness. The almond tree may also carry additional symbolic connotations that deepen the meaning – So, for example, the almond is a prolific and beautiful, blossoming tree that represents a prolific and blossoming people, as well as God's watchfulness. Unfolding the powerful, secret language of dream symbols is the key to understanding most dreams.

CHAPTER SIX

THE VARIETY OF DREAM PHENOMENON

Dreams are multifaceted experiences. Our dreams may be based in our bodies, our emotions, or our minds; but of course these aspects of our total being are connected, *"like beads on a string,"* as the Sanskrit folk-saying goes.   Although a particular dream may be rooted in our physical being, or our emotional being, or our intellectual being, or our spiritual being, most dreams encompass and artfully intertwine all these aspects of our selves. Moreover, bringing harmony to the various aspects of our selves is a primary function of the dream process.

INTERPRETING DIFFERENT TYPES OF DREAMS

Dreams are among our most intense experiences and are particularly powerful therapeutic tools. All the various approaches to dream-interpretation indicate that, what we call dreams, are not a singular phenomenon, but a broad variety of different, experiential types. Dreams include a quantitative and qualitative range of different phenomenon, only tied together by the fact that they are all mental processes, occurring while we sleep. Just as in waking life, the conscious mind carries out a broad variety of different functions like eating, speaking, walking, pondering, remembering, so too, the unconscious mind performs a wide variety of processes both physiological and psychological. We should approach our dreams

70

with the idea that there are different types of dreams, or better put, that there are a variety of different, yet related, phenomenon that we call dream. Interpretation begins by assessing what type of dream the dreamer is presenting. The basic understanding, that there are many kinds of dreams and many correlative approaches to interpretation, is the key to meaningful interpretation. Usually a dream will have a primary function, but, frequently, a single dream may fulfill several functions concurrently. Following below, I have categorized dream types in order to assist with the interpretative process, but it should be noted these categories are merely constructions serving as a general guide. More often than not a single dream will operate on more than one level simultaneously.

HYPNAGOGIC DREAMING

Hypnagogia refers to the state between Sleep and Wakefulness. It is the transition state as we enter the first phase of the dream cycle. In this phase, EEGs indicate a fluctuation between alpha and theta brainwave patterns. Hypnagogic images usually begin with the wavering, residual images of actual, sensory input from the last light that entered our retinas before we closed our eyes. They soon transform and are characterized by the uninhibited, seemingly random flow of dancing, coloured lights, as we fall asleep. Unlike our conscious thought-flow, which is primarily verbal in nature, dream-thoughts are predominantly in a non-verbal language of principally visual images, although intense sounds, smells, tastes and tactile sensations also emerge in deeper dreams.

Neurologists connect the onset of the Hypnagogic state with an electro-chemical, ocular event called a **phosphene**. A phosphene is a phenomenon characterized by the experience of seeing light, without light actually entering the eye. In the Hypnagogic state, phosphenic imagery ranges from feathery, flashing specks of coloured light, to kaleidoscopic, abstract shapes, and even to concrete, recognizable images (often faces) but usually with a ghostly appearance. As this stream of visual images dances upon our inner eye, we remain conscious but generally inattentive to the flow of our thoughts. The surge of hypnagogic imagery happens without conscious filters, and usually with very little, actual cognition. Like watching a movie in fast-forward or rewind and not really paying attention, this type of dreaming feels more like fluid thinking than actual sensorial experience. Images fly by in a seemingly random course, usually without registering a conscious or emotional response.

Some psychologists suggest that the function of this type of dreaming is mainly to sort, filter and process all the stimuli that we experience in waking life, filing some stimuli into various compartments of memory and eliminating superfluous content that has collected in our unconscious on a daily basis. Normally

Hypnagogic images act like a magic carpet that carries our thoughts as we drift off into insentient sleep.

Hypnagogic visions have been a source of inspiration for many artists and mystics, as in the popular Beatle song: *"What do you see when you turn out the light? I can't tell you but I know it's mine."* By training the mind to detachedly observe the hypnagogic flow, mystics, prophets, shamans and artists seek to enter the realm of dreams while remaining conscious. In some mystical traditions, a profound realization occurs when the observer recognizes that the dream images are self-generated.

Hypnagogic dreaming is usually the precursor of deeper, largely dreamless, sleep states, before the sleep-cycle enters the dreaming REM phase about 60 minutes later. Typically, after some 2-10 minutes, in the hypnagogic or pre-sleep phase, subjects will enter into the first stage of unconscious sleep. Gradually muscle activity slows down and brain waves move into lower frequencies as we enter into stages 2, 3 and 4. After about 60 minutes, although the body remains virtually paralyzed, our brain activity begins cycling back up into the REM phase where most dreams occur. Brain wave patterns (theta) during REM are very similar to those recorded during waking consciousness (alpha). On rare occasions, hypnagogic dreaming may transition directly into profound dream. In even rarer instances the Hypnagogic dreamer will experience a vivid, audio, visual or even tactile hallucination or visitation while still partially awake.

BODY-BASED DREAMS – ID

Body-based dreams are very common occurrences. Body dreams might better be referred to as the dreams of our animal self. This aspect of our psyche, what Freud called, the *"Id"*, instinctually seeks to satisfy our physical impulses. It is the root of our drive to survive and procreate. It is also the part of our psyche that seeks healing, sensual pleasures, self-preservation and avoidance of pain. Our animal- self encompasses all of our physical needs, desires and addictions. The specific aspect of the Id, which emphasizes our sexual drive, Freud referred to as the *"Libido"*.

The idea that, below the surface of our human consciousness, lays a wild beast, is found in many spiritual and philosophical traditions,. In the fifth century BCE, the great philosopher Socrates states, *"we each possess a lawless, wild beast nature that peers out from sleep"*. Some religious and philosophical traditions descry the beast within as selfish or evil, but, if we are to get a clear understanding of our dreams and of ourselves, we need to look at this aspect with non-judgmental eyes. Our animal nature is a vibrant and necessary vehicle for our continued life on earth. Like chimpanzees, wolves or elephants humans are social animals. Our animal-selves have an underlying impact on our social and interpersonal relationships. But humans are unlike any other animal — we have a qualitatively different, self-conscious aspect which determines the dynamic of our lives. Often our higher, self consciousness (superego) is called upon to sublimate our individual, physical drives, in order to preserve our communal, societal survival.

Although an essential, vital force, our animal aspect, when it dominates and controls our thoughts and actions, may become dangerous and destructive. It has been the mandate, of traditional religions and modern depth psychologies, to first recognize and then begin to control our unconscious, animal nature. It is important to recognize and understand our animal selves, in order to overcome neurotic and even psychotic behaviors, and to help us lead emotionally balanced lives.

Freud's classic idea that most dreams are essentially a form of ***"Wish Fulfillment"*** is highly relevant to the category of Body Dreams. His ideas, about symbolically disguising our animal desires, will prove useful when interpreting this type of body-focused dream. A primary function of dreams, involving our physical animal being, may be **to simply satisfy desires that are unavailable to us in waking life** – feeding the beast, one might say, or perhaps, *"letting the dogs run,"* says it better.

SEXUAL DREAMS – LIBIDO

Sexual dreams, where sensations and emotions often meet, are among the most common, powerful and, sometimes unsettling, dream experiences. Many clinical studies have clearly shown that both men and women regularly become sexually aroused during the REM phase of the sleep cycle. While their bodies remain otherwise paralyzed, men's penises become erect and women's clitorises and nipples swell. Heart rate and breathing also mirror the physiological patterns of waking sexual arousal. Both men and women may experience orgasm during REM sleep.

We can distinguish three categories of sexual dreams:

1) Explicit Erotic Dreams: Where the dreamer engages in, or observes, coitus or some other, overtly sexual activity. In this kind of dream the dreamer is erotically aroused and may even experience orgasm.

2) Symbolic Sexual Dreams: Explicit, sexual activity, in dreams, may also be symbolic of a non-erotic message that simply uses sex as a metaphor. Here the dreamer engages in or observes coitus or some other overtly sexual activity, but, in this kind of dream, the dreamer is **not** erotically aroused because the manifest, sexual imagery is, not actually about sex, but symbolic of some other component or idea. Sexual imagery is part and parcel of the symbolic language, with which dreams are painted, and sometimes erotic imagery does not represent an erotic idea or experience, at all. In the language of dreams, as in common colloquial, double, triple and even quadruple entendres are frequent. For example: In modern English, the primary meaning of the verb, **to screw,** is the action of turning a wedged conically shaped object used to fasten objects together. This is commonly done with a screw-driver. Another slang connotation for this verb, derived from the similar motion of the first, is the sexual act; **They screwed. = They had coitus**. Yet another meaning emerges from the first two. If one feels cheated one might say ***"so and so screwed me"***. Just so, a dream of a sexual act may really be a dream about being cheated, rather than a dream about having sex. Of course, the latent meaning of such a dream may, simultaneously, be about both sex and being cheated. For some people, this meaning of being cheated might be especially unambiguous, if one dreamt about anal sex. Yes, the uncensored language of dreams is sometimes quite rough and ready. The dictums of polite language do not apply to the unconscious – When deciphering the language of dreams, be ready for symbolic representations of direct, uncensored, unfiltered unconscious thoughts and feelings.

3) Symbolic Erotic Dreams: Where sexual activity is depicted symbolically. This is an erotically powerful category of sexual dreaming, which includes some of the most pleasurable dream experiences. With symbolic, erotic dreams, sexual activities are replaced by other activities. There are countless action substitutes for erotic love making. Some common, symbolic representations of sexual activity are: Floating, flying, race-car driving, downhill skiing, riding on a swing, and horseback riding. The genitals may also be symbolically replaced with a vast array of imagery often, but not necessarily, derived from the natural world of flora and fauna. As with slang, breasts become melons and vaginas become pussies. Most of the symbolism originates from associations based on memories of sexually stimulating experiences, which occur during childhood and early adolescence, but the process of symbol-building, by means of association, is ongoing throughout adult life.

EROTIC FANTASY vrs. SEXUAL DREAMS

Explicit, sexual dreams sometimes diverge radically from the waking, erotic fantasies of the same person. Regularly, a dreamer will find themselves engaged sexually with mysterious, forbidden, unlikely or unsuitable partners. The sexual activity itself may be unusual and seem completely inappropriate to the waking mind. In the world of dreams all *"taboos"*, to use Freud's term, vanish. Despite frequent inappropriateness and even absurdity, sexual dreams can be highly erotic experiences resulting in orgasm.

The main difference, between conscious, erotic fantasy and unconscious, erotic dreaming, is the fact that waking fantasies are directed chiefly by the conscious ego of the fantasizer, while sexual dreams are symbolic in nature, sometimes representing sublimated desires that the conscious ego is unaware of. Sexual fantasy focuses on objectifying sex partners in order to satisfy the ego's demands, while sexual dreams are the unconstrained experiencing of one's primal desires.

DREAMS OF ADDICTION

Dreams of physical addiction are very common. Depth psychologists have shown that our animal desires and lusts are featured prominently in dreams, where they often alleviate internal pressure due to repression of these natural drives. This also includes both physical and emotional addictions.

Webster's dictionary defines **addiction** as *"a compulsive need for and use of a habit-forming substance (such as heroin, nicotine, or alcohol) characterized by tolerance and by well-defined physiological symptoms upon withdrawal"*. The term, **addictions**, also includes habit-forming behaviours as well as addictive substances. Some addictions may be further defined as **self-created lusts** – that is to say they are addictions to substances or behaviours not endemic to the natural human condition, such as the normal innate desire for food or sex.

An addiction may appear, in a dream, personified as a character or other physical element. Often, but not always, the addiction will appear in the obvious guise of the actual substance, associated with the addiction. People who are in the process of withdrawing from nicotine, caffeine, alcohol, THC, or other chemical dependencies will often report vivid dreams about the substances that deliver their fixes i.e. – tobacco, coffee, liquor, cannabis etc.

On occasion an addiction, which the dreamer is not aware of, comes to light in a dream. I experienced this when, as a young student, I left my summer job at the local fast-food restaurant to return for my second year of University. At that time, I began feeling some of anxiety, not overly intense, but a gnawing, uneasy feeling. Also I was having frequent, repetitive dreams about eating fish-burgers from the fast-food restaurant where I had been working for several months. In these repetitive dreams, I am consuming the fish-burgers with acute, sensual relish, permeated with an aching sense of longing. Having already studied a little about psychoanalysis, I assumed that these dreams were probably about sex; although, at that time in my life, I was not feeling sexually deprived. The fish-sandwich dreams and the nagging anxious feeling continued for several weeks, until I finally I shared the dream privately with my psychology professor, who immediately suggested that my dream probably signaled a physical withdrawal from a substance addiction. Experience and common sense indicated to him that the culprit was probably MSG (monosodium glutamate), an addictive substance often used in fast food preparation. Although I had never heard of MSG, my physical body-consciousness intuitively knew my addiction, and exactly where I was getting my fixes. I began reading ingredients labels and then, gradually eliminating MSG from my diet. Within ten days, the fish-burger dreams and most of my anxious feelings had subsided.

Dream symbols may be woven together from various sources, drawn from personal mnemonics, from cultural references or from archetypes imbedded in the collective unconscious. A colleague of mine (call her Alice) related a dream where a fat, oversized toad jumped on her head and wrapped itself around her skull like a sticky helmet. The strange thing, in this dream, was that, initially, Alice really didn't mind the toad on her head; in fact, she rather liked the pleasant numbing sensation at first. However, she soon felt a sense of disgust and became distressed when she could not remove the toad from her head. At the time of this dream my colleague was recovering from a knee-surgery and was taking prescribed, pain medication. The sticky toad in her dream was an obvious, symbolic representation of the addictive medication and its effects. Various toads do, in fact, have glands that produce noxious substances, which act as a defense mechanism against predators. Some of these toad secretions actually have a known, narcotic effect when ingested by humans. In the popular imagination, of many cultures, the toad is associated with witchcraft, magic and poison. This, combined with the dreamer's gut reaction and personal associations, made a fat sticky toad the consummate, panoptic ideogram to represent Alice's medication and its effects. This would seem to be easily recognizable, and yet, Alice did not immediately comprehend this symbol, nor had she consciously thought much about her prescribed medication. It took a little prodding but, once she did tune into the meaning of this dream symbol, it served to inform and warn Alice about the effects and potential dangers of her medication, and she, subsequently, took action to avoid the risks.

EMOTION-BASED DREAMS, EGO

Another category, **emotion-based dreaming** is often closely linked to body-based dreams, but merges into a realm of motivations and qualities unique to human beings; what Freud referred to as *"Ego"* – a sense of oneself, and an imagining of who I am in terms of **how I see myself**, and how I perceive that others see me. As with body-based dreams, emotion-based dreams are often manifestations of wish fulfillment. They may also directly express hopes and fears, with the focus on the **dualistic** human emotions: love/hate, pride/shame, innocence/guilt, selfishness/selflessness, greed/kindness, inadequacy/superiority, jealousy/trust etc.etc. These various dualities may present ego-consciousness with some real conflicts. *"I want to be modest but I want to be sexy"*, or, *"I want to be generous but I also want to accumulate wealth."* Human life is regularly fraught with difficult, choices. Conflicting impulses, within the psyche, create stresses that can lead to emotional imbalance and even psychosis. This points toward an important function of dreams – **resolving inner conflicts and making life decisions.**

Emotionally rooted, ego dreams frequently focus on relationships with others. This type of dream will involve primary, family relationships and relationship complexes, many of which were elucidated by Freud and Jung. Dreams function, in addition to resolving inner conflicts, as **a medium for resolving situational and interpersonal conflicts.**

Ego-based dreams are the most common and highly pertinent to psychotherapeutic work. They operate in a language that is almost entirely symbolic, often difficult to decipher. Like a beautiful melody or painting, dream symbols, might express ideas that cannot be easily verbalized. They are often multi-faceted with multiple layers of meaning. Sometimes dream symbols might be deliberately disguised, like adding sweet, cherry-flavor to medicinal cough-drops, making them more palatable to our ego-consciousness. People who appear as characters in Ego dreams may represent themselves, or they may symbolize another person, or an idea, or a related memory. But most often, a character appearing in a dream symbolizes an aspect of the dreamer's own psyche, rather than an actual, other person.

LIFE-JOURNEY, CORE SOUL DREAMS

Clinical science has shown that dreaming is a universal, psychological process in humans. We have also ascertained several functions of dreaming: 1) Dreams express the fulfillment of our wishes and desires. 2) Dreams work to resolve internal and external conflicts and therefore help us make choices. **Life-journey dreaming** introduces another dimension to our dream life, which can be described as spiritual. Personal development begins to take on mythic proportions leading the dreamer on a path of self-realization. Jung touched upon soul dreaming with his ideas about the individuation process and archetypical symbols. As we have seen, **archetypes** are primary symbols that are built into the collective, human psyche. These archetypical symbols appear, not only in dreams, but also in the mythologies and stories of peoples around the world. They may be understood as sign-posts on the journey of the human soul.

Often dreams will appear to us like movies that we watch unfold in the private theatres of our minds, but with mythic or soul dreams we become fully immersed. A soul dream impacts us with the veracity of real experience, just as if happening in waking life. Many dreamers report that some of their dreams have an intensity that surpasses normal, waking consciousness. In his notes the great, Renaissance, polymath Leonardo da Vinci asks: *"Why does the eye see a thing more clearly in dreams than the imagination when awake?"*

In actual fact, Jung and many other subsequent Depth Psychologists have adopted the idea of the soul dream from the Shamanic worldview. Among tribal cultures, characterized by shamanic, religious practice, dreams are often viewed as absolutely contiguous to waking experience. Australian Aborigines and many, other, so-called primitive societies, view dreams as normal and valid events incorporated seamlessly into regular, everyday consciousness.

The Aborigines speak of the ***"Dream Time"***, understood as the past, mythic time/space continuum, when the world came into being, but also as a living dimension still accessible through dreams. For the Aborigines and many others, dreaming is seen as the very process of creation, perpetually actualizing the earth and its creatures, including humans.

Soul dreams are viewed from a number of different perspectives. Many mystical and shamanic traditions speak of a **soul-journey** and a **spirit-body**, like a vehicle in which a soul can travel to different locations in our physical world, and to other dimensions or astral planes. Other traditions characterize soul dreams as **visitations,** whereby a spirit or a message is sent from another dimension. Some of the Biblical dreams are classic examples of spiritual experiences, like the dream of Jacob from Genesis, Chapter 28:

> *"And Jacob went out from Beersheba, and went toward Haran. And he lighted upon a certain place, and tarried there all night, because the sun was set; and he took of the stones of that place, and put them for his pillows, and lay down in that place to sleep . And he dreamed, and behold a ladder set up on the earth, and the top of it reached to heaven: and behold the angels of God ascending and descending on it . . . . And he was afraid, and said, How*

dreadful is this place! This is none other than the house of God, and this is the gate of heaven."

In Jacob's dream of the ladder, with its base on earth and reaching up to heaven, his physical location does not change, but suddenly a new dimension is revealed, albeit connected to the very place. Jacob's dream does not require interpretation. It is not a symbolic representation or a retelling, but an actual event experienced while his physical body slept. Jacob, who is left shaken and in awe, immediately apprehends the tremendous implications of what he has just taken place – the Bible offers no further explanation, analysis or interpretation of Jacob's dream, leaving it to biblical scholars and mystics to distill some cogency and meaning.

MYTHS AND DREAMS

American mythologist, writer and lecturer Joseph Campbell was famously quoted as saying ***"Myths are public dreams; dreams are private myths."*** Buoyed by the ideas of Carl Jung, Campbell took archetypical symbolism, from the unconscious human psyche, into the realm of world mythology. He identified an individual's, personal, individuation process with humanity's, collective, mythic journey.

In his culminating work, <u>The Masks of God</u>, Campbell enumerates four functions of mythology which can also be readily applied to Life-Journey dreams:

1) The Metaphysical Function

This is about awakening a sense of awe before the mystery of being. Many dreams are experiences that spiritually transform the dreamer, reorienting their primary relationship with the eternal creative root of the universe. In Campbell's own words: *"The first function of mythology is to reconcile waking consciousness to the 'mysterium tremendum et fascinans' of this universe as it is."*

2) The Cosmological Function

Myths also have the function of explaining the shape of the universe. For past cultures, some myths also served as proto-science, which provided explanations on the origins and workings of the world around them. The widely-spread, Native American <u>Corn Maiden Dreams</u> (see page 29) are just one of many examples where people are provided with advanced technological knowledge through the medium of dreams. Even some modern scientists, like Dmitri Mendeleev who developed the periodic table of elements, have accredited their new discoveries to their dreams.

3) The Sociological Function

Myths also validate and support the existing social order. In order to survive societies must put into practice an existing social order, which is often validated by dreams and myths. By describing how monarchies and priesthoods are divinely ordained a society's myths and stories serve to corroborate a specific ruler or ruling group. Just so, dreams have historically been used by sovereign leaders, like the ancient Pharaohs of Egypt and the Emperors of China, to confirm their special role within the social order.

4) The Pedagogical Function

Myths provide a shared cultural reservoir that may serve as guiding models for personal growth and development. Even more so, an individual's dreams are vital, personalized guides through the stages on life's journey.

Myths like dreams can also work toward validating an individual's place within the social order, but even more significantly, myth provides a public stage unbound by social norms. Campbell refers to this mythic pattern as the ***"Hero's Journey"***. The mythic journey represents an individual's transcendence of social norms and expectations, on their way to spiritual self-realization. While myths describe famous proto-historical characters, they also represent the hero in each and every one of us.

LUCID DREAMING

Lucid dreaming is the experience of self-consciousness while dreaming. It is a dream during which the dreamer is conscious and aware that they are dreaming.

The lucid dream state provides a rarified opportunity to interact with our dreams. While lucid dreaming, the dreamer may be able to exert some degree of control over the dream narrative and environment. When the dreamer realizes that it is their own, imaginative faculty generating dream scenarios and characters, they may assert their conscious will to manipulate or redesign the dream. Losses can be turned into gains, failures into successes and defeats into wins. I recall one elderly woman, whom I worked with in one of my dream workshops. This woman, call her Linda, had given birth to a stillborn child when she was much younger. Although Linda subsequently had two, healthy children and grandchildren, she continued to regularly have nightmarish dreams wherein the stillborn child appears to her. In most of these dreams the child appears to be suffering, sometimes drowning, sometimes as if starving. Linda is horrified and does not know how to react. She would often awaken from these nightmares feeling panicked.

Many dreams, usually enveloped in intricate layers of symbolism, are dealing with unresolved loss. Dreams relating to stillbirth, abortion and miscarriage are very common themes. Understanding Linda's recurring dream about her still-born child was quite simple and straightforward. In this case, we didn't have to unravel any complex symbols. The woman's dreams were clearly expressing her need to resolve the loss of a child whom she had carried for nearly nine months, and to whom she never had a chance to say hello or goodbye. In most cases, traditional social and religious institutions provide very little in terms of a restorative, mourning processes for the mothers and fathers of miscarried or stillborn babies. It is precisely, when our conscious, waking life fails to offer a viable resolution for loss or conflict, that our unconscious will attempt healing in the realm of dreams.

The therapeutic course of action that I proposed to Linda was also very simple and straightforward. I asked her what she would say to her stillborn child if she had the chance. After discussing this in depth, I then suggested to Linda that she should find a quiet, private place, sit down or perhaps go for a walk, and imagine talking to her, stillborn child. I advised her to tell the child what she was feeling and, based on what Lucy had told me, to offer a blessing to the child. Linda did not actually follow through with my suggestion. She didn't have to. That very night she again had a vivid dream of her deceased child, but this time it was not a nightmare. In her dream Linda was able to, not only speak to her child (she knew he was a boy), but even to give him a loving hug and a blessing. She woke up throbbing with released emotion. The nightmares, which had haunted her for over forty years, stopped from that time on.

Auto-suggestion or Dream Programming techniques are used by some therapists to actually manipulate the dream content and encourage lucid dreaming towards a healing effect. Controlling dreams does have some obvious, therapeutic applications. If subjects are able to consciously interact with their dreams, then it is possible that dreams can, not only reveal the source of a psychological problem, but also provide an actual forum for resolution and healing.. But such practices do have serious limitations. Attempts at manipulating dreams will often distort and, or, dilute the power of a dream. The most powerful dreams are those that occur spontaneously, without manipulation, during the lucid state.

PAST LIFE DREAMS

The so-called Eastern religions Hinduism, Buddhism, Taoism and Jainism, together with most of the world's mystic traditions, share a belief (with variations) in the transmigration of the soul and, or reincarnation. Many dreamers report that some of their dreams seem to be memories from past lives. They recognize people and places from another life. There are several ways that past life memories might infuse our dreams:

1) A symbolic dream employs elements from past life experience. The symbol will create itself from memories that come from a past life. For example, one of my clients has recurring dreams of riding a horse. This person has come to understand that horseback riding symbolizes freedom, and sexual excitement in their personal, dream language. But strangely, this person has never ridden a horse. Where does the symbolic significance of horseback riding come from for this dreamer? Perhaps this person experienced the sensual pleasure of horseback riding in a past life.

2) The dreamer views an episode from a past life from a detached point of view, as though watching a movie.

3) An episode from a past life is vividly re-experienced. It is this last category that has provided powerful evidence for reincarnation. I have studied many uncanny cases of dreamers identifying obscure, historical details that they were unaware of before they dreamed of them.

How does one recognize and differentiate a past life dream from other dreams? In-depth analysis, of my own dreams, suggests that one of the key indicators, of a past life dream, is a sense of place – an unidentified place, yet somehow familiar, or an anonymous location that the dreamer knows and recognizes instantly. Subjects reporting past life dreams often have several, specific locations that they visit and revisit in different dreams. In addition to their familiarity, the locales of past life dreams also display features of past, historical periods and usually lack the features of current modernity.

Dreamers often meet people, in some past life dreams, whom they feel they know intimately, despite the fact that they remain unidentified to waking consciousness. Occasionally a person(s) known in current waking consciousness will appear in a past life dream, which gives basis to the widely held idea that transmigrating souls maintain karmic connections to each other for multiple lifetimes.

Critics of the reincarnation hypothesis put forward the view that such dreams do not portray elements from a past life, but are rather a product of our creative imagination. They postulate that our psyches manufacture past life scenarios, drawing from unconscious memories from one's current life. The places, that seem so familiar in dreams, may not be actual locales, but composite places designed in the dreamer's mind, using a pool of unconscious memories that have been recorded, at some point along the way, in this lifetime. Stored in their unconscious the dreamer has the data to recreate the past.

From a therapeutic point of view it doesn't really matter if one believes in reincarnation or not. I know of, at least, one Past Life therapist who is actually skeptical about the concept of reincarnation; yet she still uses the idea of past lives in her therapeutic work. This therapist uses hypnosis to regress a patient into recalling a past life. In a mild, hypnotic trance the patient will describe who they were and what they did in their past incarnations. The therapist however does not consider the material, related by his patients under hypnosis, to be actual, past-life memories. Rather she views the experiences, that her patients relate under hypnosis, to be free fantasy – the patient is relating a dream as it occurs. The therapist will interpret the past-life fantasy just as if it were a dream. Freud suggested that dream symbols are often disguises for personality aspects that the conscious ego finds unacceptable. In like manner, a subject describing themselves, in a past life, can deal guiltlessly with objectionable parts of themselves because they were part of another life or a previous incarnation. Subjects will quite candidly admit to terrible behaviour in past lives that would be unthinkable in their current life. This freedom of expression offers the therapist insight into the subject's unconscious, very much as dreams do.

Whether we consider a past-life dream experience to be a creation of our imagination, or actual vivid memories from a previous lifetime, the same interpretive and healing principles apply. But, whether or not we actually travel in a subtle body to different dimensions, or create our own worlds within our dreaming minds, the therapeutic value remains the same. As with past life dreaming, the dream will always relate to what is current in the dreamer's life. We must allow for the intuitive wisdom of the unconscious to take hold. If we have been transported back in time, by memory or by metaphysics, it is not a random trip but a journey that is specifically linked to the waking here and now. **Dreams always relate to the dreamers present life.** Whether or not, the imagery comes from the past or even from past lives

A DREAM IS ALWAYS ABOUT YOUR HERE AND NOW,
EVEN WHEN IT RELATES TO THE PAST OR FUTURE.

ASTRAL PROJECTION AND OUT-OF-BODY EXPERIENCES

Beyond the ken of standard physics, **out-of-body experiences** are generally rare occurrences that are reported by many people worldwide. Modern, paranormal researchers, in concurrence with traditional spiritualists, have linked out-of-body experiences with

astral projection. Because they occur when the body is sleeping, these experiences are studied together with dreams, but they are, by definition, a different kind of phenomenon. Whereas dreams are understood to be generated from within the unconscious mind of the dreamer, astral projection is viewed as a process whereby the soul or psyche travels out of the physical body in a subtle, high-frequency, energy body called the **astral body**. During waking hours, the astral body rests within the physical body, animating the corporeal and radiating a chromatic, energy signature, or **aura**, which surrounds the physical body. Although the aura is not immediately perceptible to most people, it is visible to many, psychically sensitive individuals, who invariably compare it to a fluctuating, multi-coloured glow emanating from and surrounding the corporeal body.

Although there is little scientific data on astral projection, there is a great deal of subjective evidence. Interestingly, the subjective evidence is highly collaborative. Descriptions of astral projection from diverse sources are remarkably similar. Most reports portray the astral body as resembling the physical body in overall structure, but of a lighter more highly-energized, less dense substance. It has been described, by mystics, as a **body of light**. The astral body is more fluid than the physical body, responding directly and immediately to thoughts and emotions, and able to transport instantaneously through space and time. The astral body usually retains a corporeal connection with the physical body. Some occultists and parapsychologists refer to this connection as **the silver cord**, envisioning a glowing, extendable cord of energy that attaches the denser, physical body to the lighter, astral body at their respective navels. The chord is a lifeline that maintains a connection to the corporeal body. If the chord is severed physical death occurs.

Multiple reports depict astral projection as flight accompanied by a sensation of power and freedom. Although some say they can astral project at will, most often, out-of-body experiences occur spontaneously, sometimes in connection with a traumatic or near-death episode. Comparing numerous similar reports gives us a general picture of the sudden, impromptu out-of-body experience. Subjects describe the initial sensation of floating in the astral body over their physical bodies. Patients on the operating table describe floating-up to the ceiling and looking down on the medical crew who are working on their bodies. One of my research subjects described such an experience: *"Imagine that you are flying a kite. It's a windy day and your kite is soaring. The kite string is tied tightly to your hand. Now imagine that your consciousness leaves your physical body and rises up, through the kite string, to the body of the kite soaring high above. You look down at your physical body far below."*

The world that the astral body travels to is often referred to as **the astral plane,** which sometimes overlaps with the physical world that our corporeal bodies relate to. Just as the astral body, when inactive, rests within the physical body, so too, the astral world rests within the physical world. The topography of the physical realm often overlies the astral world; while the astral world imbues the physical. Regularly, physical features, entities and geography coexist in more than one dimension. The tree that is growing in your back yard may also be growing in an enchanted forest on an astral plane.

Modern science has not been able to satisfactorily prove or disprove the existence of out-of-body experience and astral projection. Many dream researchers suggest that what are perceived as out-of-body experiences are, in fact, vivid dreams that occur wholly in the mind of the dreamer.

PRECOGNITIVE DREAMS

One of the most common questions people ask, regarding dreams, is: Do dreams sometimes reveal the future? It's also a question that usually comes up with a mixture of curiosity and apprehension. It's a question that is often based on an actual experience, where a dream depicts an occurrence that later is realized, or at least partially realized, in waking life. Indeed, this is a relatively common happening and, given the fact that dreams sometimes depict morbid or frightening subject matter, it's quite expected that people are uncomfortable about the possibility that dreams may foretell the future. I have identified three approaches to understanding precognition in dreams, the **Coincidental Approach**, the **Prognostic**

Approach and the **Prescient Approach**. To my way of thinking all three approaches are valid and not necessarily, mutually exclusive.

The **Coincidental** approach is based simply on numerical probabilities. Let's say there is a plane crash near a certain city. One hundred people, from that nearby city, report that they dreamt of a plane crash a night or two before it occurred. At first glance having one hundred, verified subjects reporting the same dream, just before an actual event, would suggest that there is certainly some form of premonition taking place. However, when we consider the symbolic nature of most dream imagery, and that a plane crash is a frequent, dream image (usually signifying some sort of personal disaster), we begin to see another, possible perspective. Given the fact that hundreds of thousands of people, in that same city, are each dreaming several dreams, over several hours each night, we have literally millions of dreams being dreamt on a specific night, and a probable percentage, however small, of these dreams will be about plane crashes. Whenever a major event takes place, catastrophe or triumph, it is likely that some people will dream about it, but, of course, it's just as likely that people will have these same dreams even when there is no actual corresponding event.

The second approach suggests that dreams are sometimes **prognostic**. A prognostic or **intuitive** dream is a construct, of the dreaming mind, based on probable outcomes to possible events. They do not show us what will happen, but what might happen if . . . This is to say that dreams can indeed depict and predict actual events, but not necessarily by some paranormal, psychic force, but rather based on the unencumbered workings of the unconscious mind in resolving conflicts within the psyche. In this model the unconscious has access to memories that have been abandoned or overlooked in waking consciousness. Subtle signs and hints, which are forgotten by waking consciousness, are retained and eventually processed by our dreaming mind. The dreaming mind, informed by unconscious clues, then plays-out probable scenarios. Based on this intuitive information, and bolstered by our deepest hopes and fears, our dreams may create event-based trajectories and postulate probable outcomes. For example, let's say Mary has a dream that she is fired from her job. A couple of weeks later, she is, in fact, laid off. Although she did not consciously expect to be fired, her unconscious mind may have had access to subtly cloaked insights that generated her prognostic dream. Looking back, Mary recognizes inconspicuous, nuanced changes in the behavior of her manager and some co-workers. They may have become casually distant, or perhaps overly friendly, or excessively sympathetic. Mary barely noticed these minute changes when they occurred, but she intuitively sensed that something was off beam. Her unconscious mind was able to project a plausible outcome, which in this case turned out to be true.

From my own dream-workshop experience, I have noted that another recurrent example, attributed to intuitive dreaming, is women who dream of pregnancy before it actually occurs. In many of these cases the women are wishing for and actively seeking pregnancy. But, in other cases, the women are fearful of and actually trying to avoid getting pregnant. Still other women were not consciously considering or anticipating pregnancy at all. In any case, we may allow, with each woman, that her unconscious, dreaming mind was privy to subtle, internal signals from within her body.

As we have seen, the idea, that our bodies reveal their inner workings to the dreaming mind, was articulated by ancient physicians such as Hippocrates, Galen, and others, and is still held tenable by many moderns. However, even the ancients caution that dreams are sometimes unreliable and potentially misleading, diagnostic tools. As often as not the physical condition they present has meaning widely divergent from the dreamer's actual, physical condition. Rarely does the dream of a dead body or a severed limb signify an actual physical corpse or amputation. More likely, such images will symbolize some specific, personal loss. Dreams may indeed reflect a dreamer's physical state, but they also reflect the dreamer's hopes and fears, and all this in complex symbolic language. The dreaming mind's ability to project story-lines based on subtle, physical clues can serve to warn the dreamer against possible danger but, given the nature of most dreams, they will more likely be confronting secret fears or fulfilling hidden desires, than foretelling the future.

The Third category of precognitive dreams is **Prescient Dreaming**. The 11th century physician, philosopher and Biblical scholar Maimonides, in is his famous **<u>Guide for the Perplexed</u>** says: *"dreams of the night are one sixtieth of prophecy"*. This is to say that dreams are a fraction of the same clairvoyant energy that inspired the biblical prophets with their transcendental visions. With prescient or clairvoyant dreaming we equate the dreaming mind with the mystic experience. Like the Biblical prophets or the tribal shamans, the dreaming mind must attain a state of consciousness that transcends time and space. With prescient dreaming we allow for, at least, one of two metaphysical possibilities: First, the dreamer is able to traverse linear time moving his conscious experience into the past or the future. He or she is able to actually visit the past or future from inside the experience. Second, the dreamer is able to see into the past or future from a detached, omniscient perspective, outside of the actual experience. The dreaming mind enters a mystical dimension transcending the space-time continuum, allowing for multi-directional vision into the past, present or future.

Whether experiential or visionary, clairvoyant dreams, as with most other dreams, usually take on symbolic forms to convey their multifaceted meanings. It is noteworthy that renowned clairvoyants like Nostradamus and the biblical prophets related their visions symbolically using primarily earthly elements including plants and animals.

Symbolic forms become even more essential when trying to convey realities that have no actual physical form. One of my close friends shared one of her dreams with me:

"I dreamt that I was standing on a very high mountain peak with a panoramic view overlooking never-ending valleys, meadows and hills and sparkling rivers and seas opening out below me in every direction at once, a wonderful feeling of love, tranquility and exhilaration. The dream probably lasted only a few minutes but while I was dreaming it seemed as if an eternity."

The essence of this wonderful dream does not literally include a high, mountain peak, or never-ending valleys and hills, or any other material element, but rather a direct, trans-physical experience. The high, mountain peak was my client's dreaming mind recreating her metaphysical experience into a relatable, sensory experience. Her feeling of spiritual elation had no actual physical form, but her imaginative faculty created beautiful imagery to carry the experience.

VISITS FROM THE RECENTLY DECEASED

One notable type of psychic dream, that is ubiquitous and consistently pervasive, is the **death visitation** dream. In this type of dream, the dreamer experiences a vivid, dream visit from someone, whom they are connected to. At some point, usually soon after the dream, the dreamer will discover that their dream visitor has passed on. Often the time of death will coincide closely with the time of the dream.

Like all psychic dreams, there may be various, psychological explanations for dream visits from the recently deceased, but, given their frequent and widespread incidence, such dreams are difficult to explain with purely scientific, deductive means. The corollary evidence suggests that, at the moment of death, the deceased often connects psychically with relatives and friends no matter where they are physically. Reports of dream-visits, from the recently passed, suggest that these encounters are usually very brief and of a positive, reassuring nature.

WHEN A WISH COMES TRUE

An intuitive dream may have lasting, psychological impact, especially if the true meaning is repressed. I had a client in one of my dream workshops, Wilma (not her real name), who was seeking help for anxiety and depression. Wilma related a dream that she dreamt only once, but which haunted her for over ten years. The dream occurred when Wilma was sixteen. The dream setting is in her childhood home, where she was living with her parents and older sister, except that there are secret rooms in the dream house that didn't exist in the actual dwelling. The dream narrative proceeds with Wilma gliding from room to room, and a series of strange conflicts between two floating, glowing, angel-food, birthday-cakes. The dream ends with Wilma sitting comfortably, munching on popcorn, in the passenger's seat of a parked, bright orange, convertible, sports car. She casually reads a bold, newspaper headline about some dreadful, but vague, disaster. She is startled and horrified by the newspaper headline and wakes up in a sweat.

Upon waking Wilma briefly recalled this bizarre dream, but soon forgot all about it, until several days later when something tragic brought the dream memory back with a jolt. The previous night, there had been a terrible, car crash on the highway just outside of Wilma's hometown – Wilma's older sister Jenny (not her real name), out on a Saturday night date, was killed. The family was notified by the Police at 12:00 am, and, the next morning, the fatal crash made the local newspaper. It was at the moment, when the grieving Wilma saw the newspaper headline, that her dream came back to her with vivid clarity. Straight away, Wilma intuitively connected her sister's death to this dream. Along with the recollection of the dream came a profound but irrational sense of guilt. Wilma felt that, somehow, the dream had come to warn her of the impending disaster and that she had failed to protect her sister. For the next ten years Wilma would frequently think about this dream, which was always accompanied by a vague, uneasy feeling about her sister's death. It was as though the dream was haunting her.

When she finally shared it with me, we decided to analyze the dream, gathering clues through free association and direct association. Gradually a fascinating story unfolded which finally brought closure for Wilma. The actual events went like this: Wilma and Jenny were close in age, teenage sisters, and, as is with most close teenage sisters, they were at once caring and covetous, protective and antagonistic towards each other. From an early age, the two sisters were actively competitive for the attentions of their parents. At the time of Wilma's dream, Jenny had a high-school boyfriend named James, a mop-haired lad with a shiny, blue, convertible car. Sometimes James would playfully flirt with the younger sister, just for kicks. But Wilma, just sweet sixteen, took some of it to heart and developed a crush on James. She began to fantasize about what it would be like to be James' girlfriend. Saturday night was coming up. Maybe James would ask her to the movies but, of course, not while he was with Jenny.

That night Wilma had the <u>Arguing Cakes Dream</u> which, upon analysis, proved to be about sibling rivalry, and, ultimately, her wish to remove Jenny, who seemed to be appropriating the attentions of James and, on a primal level, their parents. In the dark recesses of Wilma's unconscious was the selfish wish to eliminate her sister. It should be emphasized that this little voice of selfishness is, by no means, the dominant aspect of Wilma's personality. Wilma is, primarily, a loving and caring sister, who would never actively hurt Jenny, but, like us all, she also has an aspect that is all about satisfying her own selfish desires. Being selfish is simply a part of being human, as is being compassionate. In this case, what occurred was an unfortunate coincidence: Wilma's unconscious wish to be rid of her sister, as depicted in the dream, actually materialized with Jenny's, accidental death. Ironically Jenny was out on a date with James when she died. Unconsciously, Wilma feared that she was somehow responsible for her sister's death because she had secretly (even from her own ego-self) wished it. Unable to consciously accept the burden of guilt she repressed even the memory of this dark wish. Only the memory of the dream and a blurred sense of painful remorse came as regular reminders of profound, inner wounds. Purposively she blamed James for Jenny's death because he was the driver when the car crashed, and, unconsciously, because he was the one who had inadvertently prompted her to wish for Jenny to be gone. Her crush on James turned to vehement hatred and engendered a lasting mistrust of men in general.

Only by understanding the <u>Arguing Cakes Dream</u> was Wilma able to free herself of all these negative emotions. With great reluctance and courage, she confronted her deep unconscious fear that her selfish wish had somehow caused her sister's death. Once Wilma unraveled the meaning of her dream, she was, in due course, able to recognize that her unconscious wish to remove her sibling was a normal, relatively insignificant human emotion, and that she was truly not responsible for her sister's death. A crushing burden, one that she was not even aware that she bore, was lifted. Wilma was able to find real closure on an issue that had secretly disturbed her for years.

DISTURBING DREAMS AND NIGHTMARES

The most amazing things happen in dreams, but some dreams are unpleasant, disturbing and, sometimes, downright terrifying. Once again we have a range, of various phenomenon and root causes, for these negative experiences.

One of the biggest challenges, to the Freudian idea that dreams are primarily wish fulfilments, is the fact that some dreams are unpleasant and disturbing. People naturally ask how a nightmare could be a wish fulfillment. Freud answered this challenge by citing a series of psychological complexes like the well-known **Oedipus/Electra complexes**, wherein a child seeks to eliminate and replace the same sex parent in order to dominate a relationship with the opposite sex parent. Freud also thought there were competing drives, Death (Thanatos) and Life (Eros). He indicated that the death drive is concerned with a death wish, risk-taking and dangerous behaviour, and with a desire to return to the serenity of the womb.

Freud and Jung both recognized the dark, shadow side of the human psyche, which usually remains hidden in the unconscious. For Freud, our darkest impulses (in symbolic disguise) are satisfied in dreams, keeping them from impinging on our waking ego-consciousness. If however, while dreaming, the disguise becomes somewhat transparent, and ego-consciousness becomes partially or wholly cognizant of actual, latent content, the dreamer might be horrified at the apprehension of their own sinister wishes – a nightmare could ensue.

Although Freud's wish-fulfilment explanation for nightmares often holds true, most Depth Psychologists, including myself take a broader approach, which draws on both Freudian and Jungian ideas. In Jungian thought, the elements in a dream are not disguised but symbolically revealed. It is confrontation, with our own shadow-self, that can terrify us.   Nightmares bring us face to face with our darkest fears. Nightmares and disturbing dreams often point to conflicts within the psyche. They may also be mechanisms for dealing with past traumatic experiences, and preparing for future ones.

We can identify four main categories of negative dreaming:

i) Distressing Dreams,

ii) Nightmares,

iii) Sleep Terrors,

iv) Parasomnia

DISTRESSING DREAMS

Distressing dreams usually do not wake the dreamer from sleep and are not necessarily terrifying, but rather disquieting and often confusing. This type of dream occurs during the Rapid-Eye-

Movement stage of sleep and is often recalled upon waking, however usually the recall is somewhat vague. A distressing dream may leave the dreamer with an unsettled feeling when they awake, and this feeling sometimes filters into the dreamer's mood throughout that day.

NIGHTMARES

Nightmares are dreams, with vivid and terrifying content, usually leading to immediate awakening. The dreamer will usually have vivid recall upon waking from a nightmare, and, although this memory might soon be forgotten, they are, sometimes, remembered for many years. These frightening experiences occur in the REM (Rapid Eye Movement) stage of the sleep cycle, usually in the later hours of sleep.

Nightmares are most common in children but are also experienced by adults. A person awakened from a nightmare will usually have a clear recollection of the dream narrative. Children often describe being chased by a monster or a wild beast or, most horrifying of all, a nameless darkness. Nothing is more terrifying than the unknown. Adults describe their bad dreams in an infinite array of dreadful, complex scenarios. Nightmares may occur during a troubled time in an individual's life, or as the result of a deeply emotional or traumatic event.

Although considered a normal occurrence, that most people experience intermittently, research has shown that frequent and repeated nightmares may be symptomatic of Post-Traumatic Stress Disorder (PTSD), Generalized Anxiety Disorder (GAD), Depression, Bipolar Disorders and Narcotic Use. These exceptional nightmare situations differ from other nightmares in that they do not necessarily occur in REM sleep, but may come on in any of the stages of sleep.

SLEEP TERRORS

Often confused with nightmares, sleep-terrors are a distinct phenomenon, most common in, but not exclusive to, children. Unlike nightmares, sleep- terrors occur in the deep, non-REM stages of sleep. Typically the subject is aroused from sleep in a state of extreme agitation, often screaming, sweating and with dilated pupils. After several moments of apparent, unmitigated terror the subject will suddenly relax and return to deep sleep. Unlike nightmares, the subject does not seem to be fully awake when aroused and will usually have absolutely no immediate or later recollection of the episode or of a related dream.

MEMORIES OF BEING BORN AND OF DYING

Little is known about the cause of sleep terrors but I suggest that these occurrences relate to memories of being born. It is well known that unborn babies, in the third trimester, experience REM (rapid-eye-movement) while sleeping in the womb. It is a time when trillions of neural connections are formulating in the developing brain, providing the physical seat of memory and consciousness. Some **Dreamologists** (psychologists who work with dreams) insist that the content, of some dreams, is actually prenatal, reflecting the earliest experiences and sensations of a developing consciousness. The actual process of birth is often a traumatic shock for the infant, who is being thrust, from its warm, floating existence in the womb, into a series of violent contractions, down a constricted tunnel and finally into an unknown universe of blaring sounds, blinding lights, cold air and oft-times a stinging slap on the behind. The traumatic memory of birth, embedded deep into the unconscious, before the individual has formulated a self-image or ego context, could incite these nameless horrors. Indeed sleep terrors appear to be the re-experience of extreme fear without rhyme, reason or any context. Prenatal and birth experiences may also precipitate the new-born's first awareness of **self and other**. Becoming conscious that one is separate, from the rest of the universe, is terrifying on a primal level.

We have already discussed Past Life dreaming, in a previous chapter, and how pleasant and unpleasant experiences, from a previous incarnation, might be relived in dreams. Some of those, whom I've interviewed, reported dreams of being wounded and dying on a battlefield, or in some other dangerous situation. Many others dream of being attacked and murdered in a variety of realistic, yet anachronistic settings. When it comes to extreme nightmares and sleep-terrors, the specific memory of dying stands out. The moments immediately preceding death, like the moments of birth, are often particularly traumatic. Because the moment of death involves the disintegration of a body-based, self identity, sleep-terrors based on a non-contextual memory might ensue. When one apprehends that the physical body, with which they identify, is no longer alive and that they are no longer attached to it, a feeling of nameless panic could ensue. These moments of being totally lost and alone may resurface in episodes of sleep-terror.

Similarly, some parapsychologists suggest that sleep terrors and some nightmares are related to out-of-body experiences. The common **dream of falling**, which most people recall experiencing at least once, is also connected to the dream body or astral body returning to its physical body. Mystics and shamans, familiar with out-of-body experiences, advise extreme caution when traversing the astral realms. Shamanic, dream travelling usually requires special training and preparation, but such experiences also occur spontaneously in unpracticed individuals including young children.

When a sleeping individual becomes aware of themselves, in an out-of-body state (as in lucid dreaming), they may react with extreme disorientation and panic. An out-of-body experience can shatter one's ego-based self-image, resulting in existential terror. This primal fear may arise with the sudden recognition of complete aloneness, lost in a universe where nothing is familiar. It is, at once, deep darkness and dazzling light, terrifying and euphoric.

PARASOMNIA PHENOMENON

The fourth category of disturbing dreams includes a number of unusual, sleep phenomenon: **Somnambulism** (moving while asleep)**, Somniloquy** (sleep-talking)**, Post-Traumatic Nightmares, Sleep Paralysis and REM Behavior Disorder (RBD).** All of these experiences occur during NREM (non-rapid eye movement) sleep, except for Sleep Paralysis and REM Behavior Disorder, which occur during the transition phase from REM to awakening. Post-traumatic nightmares can occur any time during the sleep cycle.

Sleep-Paralysis is most often experienced when a person becomes conscious, just as they wake up from REM, but find themselves unable to move or speak. Similar paralysis also occurs, though rarely, during a lucid dream or while falling asleep. Sleep Paralysis is experienced, by most people, at least once in their lives, but is sometimes much more frequent. Normally our physical body remains relatively still during REM sleep, while our dream-body (our dream persona) participates in a wide variety of actions. This is due to the phenomenon of **REM-atonia;** whereby all voluntary muscle control is immobilized during REM sleep. The REM-atonic condition normally acts as a defense mechanism, so that dreamers are not physically acting out their dreams. Sleep paralysis occurs during the transition from REM to waking consciousness, as a lingering effect of REM-atonia.

Episodes of sleep paralysis generally last for several minutes. The sudden awareness of paralysis, sometimes, brings about feelings of panic and helplessness. Often sleep paralysis is accompanied by audio or visual hallucinations. Subjects hear strange sounds, sometimes whispering voices. Many report the unnerving awareness of an intruder in the room with them.

Sometimes the experience of sleep paralysis has overtones of a forced, sexual encounter that the paralyzed individual is helpless to repel. Like the medieval Succubus and her male counterpart the Incubus, malevolent, otherworldly creatures are, time and again, described as squatting on a sleeping person's chest, creating an impression of invasive, suffocating pressure, and usually inducing a fearful reaction. In recent times similar accounts continue and are commonly associated with reports of **alien visitations and abductions**.

During a sleep paralysis episode, fear often escalates into panic, exasperated by the person's inability to move or speak, or even to audibly cry out. Thankfully, sleep paralysis episodes are typically brief, dissipating as the person becomes fully awake. Occasionally the subject will fall back into a deep sleep. Sleep paralysis is not always unpleasant however, and is sometimes experienced as a pleasant floating sensation closely aligned with out-of-body experiences.

Occurrences of **Somnambulism** (sleep walking and moving during NREM sleep), although quite common, are usually isolated and non-repetitive, but some individuals do have frequent episodes, which can lead to dangerous incursions into their exterior environment. One of my research subjects had several somnambular incidents where he got out of bed, walked into his living room, urinated on his television set, and returned to bed. In the morning he had absolutely no recollection of the event. This happened on three occasions within a 30 day period (witnessed each time by his roomate). Thankfully, the behaviour stopped as suddenly as it had begun.

A specific form of somnambulism is **Sexsomnia,** which refers to active, sexual behaviours during sleep. Sexsomnia occurs during NREM sleep, when sleeping individuals engage in sexual behaviours such as masturbation, oral sex, fondling, and even intercourse. The activity is unconscious and dream recall is extremely rare. Little is known about this phenomenon, but recent studies have shown that it is much more common than previously thought. One study done by the Sleep Research Laboratory at the University Health Network's of Toronto Western Hospital, in 2010, estimated that 11% of men and 4% of women, who were patients at their sleep clinic, reported experiencing at least one episode of Sexsomnia. Studies also indicate that most cases of sexomnia occur with relationship partners who share a bed and are rarely reported. According to the International Classification of Sleep Disorders, published in 2005 by the American Academy of Sleep Medicine, *"Sexsomnia appears to occur predominantly during confusional arousals and may occur during an episode of sleepwalking."* Confusional arousals usually happen without the sleeping person becoming consciousness. An individual, who has undergone a sexomniatic occurrence, will typically awaken with absolutely no memory of the episode. There is much ongoing, medical and legal debate about the nature of Sexsomnia, which has been used, on rare occasions, as a criminal defence in alleged, sexual assault cases.

THE ELUSIVE SEARCH

Despite their unpleasantness, negative dreams and nightmares, when interpreted and analyzed, are exceedingly useful to the therapeutic process. For example, one very common, dream theme is the **Elusive Search.** In this sort of dream something is lost, missing or forgotten, and the dreamer is searching, but the missing something is not found and remains frustratingly elusive. Emotions in this type of dream can range from mild anxiety to outright panic. These dreams tell us that we are searching for something, but what could it be? Analyzing the elements of the dream, using the methods laid out in this book, will help us define what it is that we are searching for. What am I looking for? Am I searching for love, searching for success, searching for security, searching for the right path to take, searching for meaning, etc. etc.?

In my personal version of the Elusive Search dream, I am searching high and low for my keys. When I analyzed this element, together with other elements in the dream, I came to better understand just what it was that I was seeking, at the time in my life when the dream occurred. Everything became clearer when I understood what *"the lost keys"* symbolically represented to me.

ARCHETYPICAL LEARNING: PREPARING FOR CRISIS

Freud and many subsequent psychologists focus on the idea that dream symbols are generated solely by the creative imagination of the individual.   An alternative approach ties in closely with Carl Jung's ideas about the collective unconscious, and may help us better understand some of our unpleasant dreams. This approach postulates that we genetically inherit some of our dreams. The idea is put forward that certain, perilous situations, which were actually experienced in the lives of our early human ancestors, have been embedded into our collective unconscious, and into our DNA. These inherited experiences are replayed in our nightmares especially those of children. So, for example, a young child, who has never actually seen a wolf, will dream of being chased by one. Indeed it is common, for modern urban-dwellers of all ages, to dream of animals they have not actually encountered. According to some anthropologists, the nightmares of our early ancestors operated as a survival mechanism. The original function of such nightmares is to prepare the dreamer for possible, real encounters with such dangers in waking life. By rehearsing, in the simulated world of dreams, defensive strategies could be developed and used when confronted with similar occurrences in waking life. Although most modern humans do not have to worry about being hunted by wolves, the primitive imagery remains in our dreams.

Perhaps these primal images are still relevant to moderns because such images, like a wolf, a snake, a lion, a flood, a fire, a storm etc., have taken on potent, symbolic, positive and negative connotations. When we dream of being chased by a beast, like a wolf, we may very well be learning to deal with the ravenous, internal and external negative forces which attack us in our everyday lives. The stresses and perils of modern life are reconfigured to assume the forms of nature's primal elementals. These shared, archetypical symbols are derived from the earth, which spawned humankind, and have become integrated into each individual's, self-created, dream language.

CHILD'S PLAY/ WAKING DREAMS

Watch very young children playing, and you will see conscious and unconscious wishes and desires being dreamed-out before your eyes. It is fascinating how easily children can transpose their conscious reality, from the physical world into a world of fantasy that they create themselves. Even more remarkable is the ability of children to share, assimilate and integrate each other's fantasies, while playing together. Anyone, who has ever observed children at play, will attest to the fact that sometimes a child will come into serious conflict with their playmates in a universe created solely through their shared imagination. Real, heartfelt conflicts can arise based on wholly imaginary events in a fabricated world.

Swiss psychologist Jean Piaget, an outstanding figure in modern cognitive psychology, examines the connection between children's play and dreams and their key role in cognitive development including perception, learning, reason, memory, language and imagination. In his chief study of children's dreams, <u>Play, Dreams and Imitation in Childhood</u>, first published in 1946, Piaget discusses how children adapt to the world around them through two basic strategies: ***"accommodation* and *assimilation"***. Accommodation is basically achieved through repeated imitation of what a child has observed, in an attempt deal with objective reality. Assimilation, on the other hand, is basically achieved through play, where children can create and control their own realities and their own subjective desires and wishes. Dreams, in this view, are largely a continuation of the kind of symbolic play that comes so naturally to young children. Both dreaming and play are essential to healthy, cognitive development. Both dreaming and playing articulate a child's, primary, physical and emotional fears and wishes (conscious and unconscious), and both dreams and play are expressed symbolically. Nightmares mark a divergence between play and dream because, in dreams, the individual has generally less control over deep-seated, unconscious matter. It is a balanced correlation between the subjective and objective realities of the developing child, achieved with the help of dreams and play, which eventually leads to a well-adapted, functional and creative adult.

WELCOME TO WONDERLAND

For each of us dreaming is an active ongoing process that is part of our everyday lives, though we are often unaware of it. Figuratively speaking, the diaphanous wall which separates our controlled, waking consciousness from the wild, untamed worlds of our unconscious, sometimes breaks down and cracks under pressure. In special circumstances, such as post-traumatic or age-related brain disease, our dreams may seep through the cracks from the depths our unconscious into our waking life. For some this invasion from dreamland is a temporary episode of delirium; for others it's episodic, coming and going, and, for some, it remains a chronic condition.

It is fascinating to see how our minds can blend the world of our dreams with our waking consciousness. I have seen many cases of patients waking up after surgery still fully dreaming, yet interacting with the waking world. It is as if they were enhancing their perception of physical reality with imaginary additions and enhancements. I recall one woman having an animated conversation with her bedside nightstand, which she imagined was her grandson. Another man, awakened after heart surgery, believed he was in a fancy, hotel restaurant. He became quite upset when the waitress/nurse attempted to insert an IV tube and demanded to speak with the hotel-manager, but, despite his indignation, the man did not recognize the illogic and absurdity of his situation.

Delusional episodes are also common accompaniments to various forms of dementia. I have observed this closely with a number of people. Usually, at some point the person will return to their past – speaking their first language or singing a long-forgotten, childhood lullaby. I have been privy to a vast range of fascinating, delusion scenarios that accompany various forms of dementia. One patient, whom I visited in a nursing home, consistently believed and acted as if he was in charge of operating a major, international airport. Each day, from his wheel chair, he would direct imaginary employees (often his care-givers and nurses) through a series of intricate, operational scenarios landing planes and dealing with highjackers and other aviation emergencies. This man, by the way had no previous experience working at an airport, but he did find his imaginary work very self-gratifying and esteem building. We often mistake the delusions, strange actions and weird speech of people with dementia as being the meaningless, shattered pieces of a broken mind, but, if we look and listen closely, even in these extreme circumstances, we can see the healing power of dreams at work providing comfort and resolution of interior conflicts for the storm-tossed soul.

CHAPTER SEVEN

DREAM KEEPER

MEMORIES OF NOW

Stored within our unconscious are recordings of our past experience. Parapsychologists and some psychologists suggest that, in fact, all of our life experience is recorded and stored within the unconscious. Various mystic and religious theorists even suggest that memories, from previous lives or incarnations, are also to be found in the hidden, memory vaults of our minds. When unconscious records of past experiences are processed through conscious thought, they become memories. Research suggests that much, if not all, of an individual's dream imagery derives from their past experience.

Occasionally a dream memory will appear **in context** – that is to say it will feel as though one is truly viewing or re-experiencing an actual episode from the past. But, most often, images, from the past that we re-experience in a dream, appear **out of context**, like random pieces from different puzzles. Such dreams are masterfully assembled collages, created from diverse scraps of unconscious memory, and reassembled into totally new experiences.

Dreams will often present us with vivid images from past experiences that have long since disappeared from waking consciousness. In dreams one will sometimes view, with absolute clarity, the face of someone or something long forgotten to conscious

123

recollection. In one of my own recollected dreams, I meet a certain young woman whose face and voice I clearly recognized, though upon waking I had no idea who this woman was. I was momentarily intrigued by this familiar, yet unidentified character, but soon forgot about it. It happened, quite by chance that, a few weeks after I had this dream, I was perusing through my family photo album, and came upon my kindergarten class picture – There, standing in the back row beside the teacher, was the young woman I had seen in my dream. I asked my mother about her, and was surprised to find that she did, in fact, remember the young woman very clearly, although she could only recall her first name, Jen. She was the kindergarten teacher's assistant, but, most notably, my mother recalled that Jen babysat for me on the day my grandfather passed away, while she and my father went to make funeral arrangements. I was five years old at the time. I still have a vague memory of that day; seeing my mother cry for the first time. For me, all conscious memory of Jen had disappeared, but she remained in my unconscious memory-bank, only to re-emerge thirty-five years later, clear as day, in a dream. However my dream was not just a replay of a memory from my early childhood. The image, stored within my unconscious memory, did not randomly surface. The memory of this young woman was transformed into an evocative and redolent symbol. In the secret world of my unconscious, she had taken on meaning – meaning pertinent to my life at the time of the dream. Significantly, this dream of mine occurred around the time that my own father passed away. With strong associations to my grandfather's passing and my first, personal encounter with death, the memory of this long forgotten person was incorporated into my own, private, dream dialect. My creative unconscious had made an obscure connection, which linked my emotional response to my grandfather's death when I was five years old, to my father's death 35 years later. But how and why does the psyche make these artful connections, fashioning complex, idiomatic language?

The healing force of a memory-based dream resides in the psyche's imaginative and creative power. Not only is our unconscious able to recreate a past experience, but our psyche can also create a new reality by transforming the old. Just as with out-of-context dreams, where bits and pieces of past experience might be reassembled into something completely new, so too, with in-context dreams where one relives an actual, past event. By revisiting a past experience, our psyche provides itself with an opportunity to reassess and learn from experience. It is important to note that these dreams from the past, occur in relation to a situation that is current in an individual's, waking life. For example, one may be faced with a difficult, life choice. The psyche's unconscious search for harmony generates dreams in which a similar, hard choice, from a past experience, presented itself. In essence we are learning from experience – the dream provides the experience, either by manufacturing a parallel, new experience, or recreating a past event, albeit symbolically transfigured. The psyche draws parallels to similar life situations, applying past experience to current, ongoing situations. Remember: it's always about your here and now! Whatever variety of dream one experiences, count on the fact that it is connected to a current situation in the dreamer's life. Dreams reflect an individual's **present** life and state of being, and are an active expression of life's ongoing changes.

Even dreams of different types (including dreams of the past) have, in common, this dynamic connection to the here and now. Let's look at an actual example of two, different dreams, to see how they both reflect the current life of the dreamer. Both dreams were dreamt by the same subject within a couple of days of each other. The subject, Joan (not her real name), is a woman, aged twenty eight, a single, working mother of two children whom she is struggling to support on a meager income.

The first dream: Although she is the main character, Joan experiences this dream as a detached observer. *"I see myself in a tiny broken down, one-room house. In the house, I am riding a small, wobbly tricycle, suitable for a young child, and my two kids have climbed up onto my back and shoulders. I feel a great weight, and a dreadful fear of losing my balance and crashing to the floor with my children. I feel like an observer watching this scene from outside. I felt upset by the pathetic, ridiculousness of the scene I was seeing."*

The second dream: The next night Joan experiences this brief, but vivid, dream. This time her point of view is not as an observer, but rather, she is fully immersed in the dream as if it were occurring in waking consciousness. *"In this dream, I am marching along a rough, dirt road with many other weary, bedraggled people. It is winter, and blizzard force winds are stinging my cheeks as I plod along, feeling great weariness and heaviness of heart, against the freezing wind and snow. Beneath my threadbare cloak, I clutch my swaddled, baby daughter in my arms, trying desperately to keep her warm. I am aware that the baby I am carrying is my actual, eldest daughter in waking life although she is, in reality, now eight years old, but I know that it is her. The icy wind howls as I walk on, cradling the child to my breast. As I walk along my heart is throbbing with love for the child I carry, and an unshakeable, desperate determination to save her."*

Joan's two dreams are obviously very different. They have different content, different feelings, different structures and different points of view. The first dream was a symbolic representation of her current state of being. It was as if her unconscious had provided a cartoon (though not funny) to clearly reflect her present, apparently futile situation. It contained absurd and irrational elements that only make sense when understood symbolically. The tiny tricycle represented the inadequate vehicle or support system with which Joan was desperately trying to manage her life. The fact that it was a child's tricycle, referred to Joan's own immaturity and lack of experience in dealing with her current responsibilities (the children climbing on her shoulders). Indeed this dream did offer a precise, symbolic representation of Joan's fears about her situation at that time. Seeing herself precariously balanced on the tiny tricycle, with her children clinging to her back and shoulders, evoked a complex amalgam of mixed emotions: frustration, helplessness, shame, resentment, anger, fear, struggle and a sense of being violated and abused. Naturally, recalling this dream left Joan with an unsettling feeling of apprehension and depression.

The second dream had no irrational elements – It depicted a poignant scene that could have actually occurred. Interestingly, Joan recognized the second dream, not as a construct of her imagination like the first dream, but as an actual memory from a past life (she believed it showed an historic, forced migration that occurred during some past war). But, whether or not this was, in reality, a past life memory, the dream did **not** occur randomly, rather it manifested or re-manifested at a precise time in Joan's life. I worked with Joan on these two dreams: We determined that the first dream's primary function was to show Joan the precariousness of her current situation. This dream leaves Joan shaken, depressed and questioning her future.

The second dream comes as if in answer to the first. It pointed towards the emotional strength that Joan needed to muster in order to make the journey. In the dream, and in her life, Joan's source of strength is her love for the child that she carried. The Joan in the second dream is not the weak, inept failure of the first dream, but a strong, devoted woman determined to save her beloved children in the face of great adversity. The second dream gave Joan the reassurance that she in fact did possess the strength to make it. The two dreams, although quite different in nature, worked together providing insight, emotional release and support at a difficult juncture in this person's life.

REMEMBERING AND FORGETTING DREAMS

Most people experience long periods where they do not recall their dreams, or, if they do recall them, they don't pay much attention to them, and this is as it should be. As with our other autonomic processes, such as breathing and digestion, we don't usually pay them much conscious attention, unless a problem occurs. After all, when we are awake, we should focus primarily on the here and now of our waking world. There is ordinarily no need to chase after dreams, although some people enjoy an active dream life, meaning they often recall and record dreams, and benefit from meditating on and analyzing them. Others do not focus on their dreams, preferring to allow their unconscious activities to remain in the shadows, while they concentrate on the immediate concerns of waking life. Both are healthy attitudes and one should do what comes naturally, not forcing a conscious preoccupation with dream life, nor turning away from our dreams when they call to us.

Many psychologists, who work with dreams, stress the importance of remembering dreams and remembering them accurately. My approach differs somewhat from this mainstream thinking. With memories, in general, and especially with dream memories, the membrane between conscious and unconscious is quite diaphanous. Memories spontaneously surface into consciousness, and memories spontaneously slip away into unconsciousness. The question is; whether or not the moments of remembering and the moments of forgetting occur randomly, or in conjunction with a person's present situation. Most Depth Psychologists would agree that, when a dream is extremely vivid and or repetitive, hanging around in one's thoughts for a long time, then it's time to pay attention to the message the unconscious is sending. This is especially true when a person is experiencing neurotic or psychotic emotions or behaviour, signaling an unconscious, psychological conflict. A safe and effective way to reach into the unconscious and uncover such conflicts is through analyzing dreams.

BURIED TREASURE - RECALLING OLD DREAMS

Some dreams stay with us for life. Although it is best to record a dream as soon as possible after awakening, recording a previous dream, at a later time, is also a valuable endeavor. Most of us can readily recall, at least partially, one or several dreams we have had throughout our lives. Other dream memories hide, in the shadows of our pre-conscious and unconscious for long periods, until a moment when they suddenly re-emerge. Moments later these same, mnemonic snippets might retreat again into the dark recesses of forgetfulness.

Imagery and settings from past dreams are very often recurrent. Sometimes a dream, or a similar, parallel dream, recurs days, weeks or even years later, and, curiously, we recall that we've had this dream before. One may have the sense that they are revisiting a familiar place that they have visited before. I have often listened to the recollections of dreams that were dreamed many years earlier, often from childhood or adolescence.

Try right now, as you read these words, to recall and visualize a dream, or at least a brief moment from a dream that you've had sometime throughout your life. Chances are you, like most people, will find that the dreams you recall are not the most recent, but dreams you've dreamt some time ago. The dreaming psyche, like the dream, is ageless. Ironically these abiding dreams, that we evoke throughout our lives, are often the most difficult to describe because they are in a primal language that only the dreamer's, deepest consciousness fully understands. But re-examining these old dreams can be enlightening. I have seen many cases where a new, clearer understanding of an old dream comes to light when the dream is revisited much later. Some old dreams may be among our most treasured memories.

ENHANCING RECALL

Auto-suggestion is the basic technique used, by most therapists, to increase accurate recall. There are many variations on this primary method for recalling and recording one's dreams. As you drift off to sleep you can give yourself an auto-suggestion by repeating the suggestion, over and over, a number of times. You may repeat the suggestion internally or vocalized. Attune your attention to the suggestion as you repeat it. Actively listen to your own voice, or inner voice, as you make the suggestion. For example one might repeat to oneself: ***"I will remember my dreams when I wake in the morning! I will remember my dreams when I wake in the morning. . ."*** over and over, ten or twenty times.

Auto-suggestions can also be more specific and explicit . For example, one may autosuggest a distinct type of dream or a specific subject. For example: ***"I will dream about my career path tonight,"*** or, ***"I will dream about my love life tonight. . ."*** Some prefer to pose the auto-suggestion as a general or particular question. For example: ***"How can I find happiness?"*** or ***"Should I take on a new job or relationship?"*** or ***"What colour car should I get?"*** or . . . Autosuggestion may not work every time, but despite its simplicity, with a little practice, this method is often effective both for dream recall and, to a lesser extent, for directing dreams.

Beyond the ken of the average dreamer, there are, in addition, rigorous, meditation techniques analogous to methods used by Shamans, Yogis, Sufis, Kabbalists and other mystical practitioners. More complex, auto-suggestion or **Dream Programming** techniques are also used by lucid dreamers to control dream content. As we have seen, some therapists use the lucid dream state to allow dreamers to manipulate the contents of their dreams towards a healing effect. The drawback to dream programming or manipulation, however, is that this practice will likely distort the original, unconscious experience. My own approach prefers and allows for the spontaneous, non-interventionist experience of dreams.

Rather than seeking out your dreams, let your dreams find you.

RECORDING DREAMS

For recording dreams the best method is writing them down or audio recording, as soon as possible, upon waking. Keep that pen and pad, or recorder, at your bedside. Make a conscious effort to avoid distorting the dream record, writing freely without any pre-analysis or spontaneous reinvention, no matter how bizarre or even offensive, the dream content may seem. Most often the recollection of a dream will dissipate, becoming vague or completely forgotten within a few moments of awakening.   It's advisable to record promptly.

DRAWING YOUR DREAMS

Because dreams tend to be visual, rather than verbal, sketching is a helpful way to record a dream. Drawing is often used by child-psychologists in order to discover a child's emotions, which are frequently difficult to articulate verbally. As with writing down a dream, the drawing should be done as soon as possible upon waking. When recording a dream with a

drawing, one should be unconcerned with the artistic quality or composition. The major elements of the dream should be quickly sketched out with as little hesitation as possible. Drawings may be little more than scribbles, but they can be effective records of a dream. In addition, drawings will often include visual details that a verbal description may omit.   They may  depict some, bizarre realities that are difficult to relate in words.

Dream sketches are sometimes reworked by artists to create finished works. There are innumerable works of visual art and literature that have been inspired directly by dreams. In fact it, could be argued that all art is rooted in our unconscious.

DRAMATIC IDENTIFICATION WITH A DREAM ELEMENT

One of the most cathartic ways to penetrate the essence of a dream is through dramatic identification with a specific, dream element (person, animal or thing). This therapeutic technique was largely developed by the German-born psychiatrist and psychotherapist Frederick (Fritz) Perls. Perls was one of many who walked boldly through the doors that Freud and Jung had opened, adding his own perspective to the therapeutic use of dreams. According to Perls, people suffer psychologically because of ***"self-alienation – disowning parts of ourselves"***. The goal of his ***"Gestalt"*** therapy is to reclaim disowned or impoverished aspects of ourselves and reintegrate them into our whole personality. *"Dreams are existential experiences, created by, and of, and for the dreamer."* This therapeutic approach works on the premise that: **every element in a dream is actually an aspect of the dreamer**. Perls states that: *"In Gestalt therapy we don't interpret dreams. We do something much more interesting with them. Instead of analyzing and further cutting up the dream, we want to bring it back to life"*. (Perls, F. S. (1969). Gestalt Therapy Verbatim.)

The dramatic identification, using the Dream-Selfie method, begins with first recognizing elements in a dream, and then going on to identify with individual elements through role play. The dreamer describes the dream in the present tense, as if it was occurring in the moment, and then goes on to role-play a specific element of the dream. For example, one dreams of encountering a frightening bear. Like an actor assuming a dramatic role, become the bear. Identify with the thoughts and feelings of this bear and describe them. As the bear, do you feel angry, or curious, or hungry, or powerful, or hostile, or friendly etc.? Say out loud what you are feeling and thinking as you invoke the specific element.

It is particularly helpful to have a trusted dream-guide when working with this technique. A guide can serve as an audience, which the dreamer can play to, when acting-out a dream element. A dream guide should also write down significant details. If you are working without a guide, you may want to have a recording device so that you can reflect on your dramatic recreations later, without interrupting the ongoing process. Even without a guide, assuming the role of a dream element often brings deep insights. I have included a Gestalt inspired exercise, as an optional step, in the <u>DREAM SELFIE GUIDE</u> coming up in part II. This exercise is optional because this method may be too intense or awkward for some individuals.

TO SHARE OR NOT TO SHARE/ YOUR PRIVATE WORLD

Sharing dreams with a group is a common-place feature of many cultures, both historic and modern. Examples of communal dream-sharing can be found among many tribal societies. Within some of these traditional communities, it is a customary practice to share one's dreams with a shaman, a small group of elders, or even with the whole, village community, especially when seeking healing from some kind of crisis or affliction. Dreams are also regularly shared, more privately, within family groups or with friends.

Not all tribal peoples share dreams so readily, however. Among some cultures, like the Hopi and Zuni of New Mexico, most dreams are not shared. Hopi only share bad dreams, with the idea that sharing the dream is a way of purging the negative energy it may hold. Positive dreams are not shared, but kept *"in the heart"* so that their power is not dissipated – something like the modern North American custom of keeping your wish secret after blowing out the candles on a birthday cake.

There are many psychologists and psychotherapists today, who find group dream-sharing to be a therapeutic and cathartic process. Sharing dreams, in a secure group setting with the help of a trusted guide, has several therapeutic benefits. By sharing, in the context of group therapy, a participant can unburden themselves, as one unburdens themselves with an admission or a confession. In addition, a participant may also receive support and direction from the group whose participants share a common issue or problem. It becomes easier to face a dilemma when we feel we are not alone, and that others share our same concerns. Although dream sharing, with a support group or with friends and family, offers potential for catharsis and subsequent healing, there are also some limitations when it comes to interpreting a dream down to its core. For one thing, the recounting of a dream, within the context of a support group, will almost certainly be distorted to some degree. Just sharing a dream, even with a therapist, will usually fudge the meaning of that dream to some extent. In order to protect our ego's self-image, it's a natural tendency, often unconscious, to alter some features of a dream, in the telling. Also the interpretation of a dream, shared with a group, will usually be misdirected towards the specific concerns of that group, which may or may not be the primary meaning of the dream.

There are times in waking life when we require complete privacy. Even more so with dreams, when we are totally alone – no one is watching, no one is judging. The secrets we find, hidden within our dreams, may remain hidden – Nature has sealed our ultimate right to privacy. We are each given a private, internal world, which only we can truly understand. This, in fact, is the primary reason for this book – providing the tools to unreservedly interpret, each their own dreams, in the privacy of their own minds. Dreams are our most personal of experiences – beyond what even highly-sophisticated, vocabular language can convey; they belong only to the dreamer. IT'S OK TO **NOT** SHARE; in fact, often it is preferable.

PART II
THE DREAM-SELFIE METHOD
STEP BY STEP GUIDE

BEFORE YOU BEGIN

Ultimately it is the dreamer alone who can truly interpret their own dreams, although this is often more easily accomplished with the assistance of a dream specialist who is able to guide the dreamer on their journey of self-discovery. By following this, step by step, guide you can begin to interpret **your** own dreams, without the help of specialist.

Sometimes the unconscious provides a guide within the dream itself. It's fairly common to have someone – a wise person or spirit guide – appear in a dream, pointing you in the right direction or offering some light in the darkness. Whether you are working with a therapist or on your own, I invite you, the reader, to use this book as a guide for exploring and analyzing your dreams. Interpreting one's own dreams, without a guide, is certainly doable, but it presents some specific challenges. Below are some possible pitfalls to be aware of when interpreting your own dreams.

BE PREPARED FOR THE UNEXPECTED

Accurate dream analysis is not something that can be done with a dictionary of dream symbols or a lexicon of ready-made interpretations. Occasionally, such prefab, interpretation tools can provide helpful hints, but they can also be misleading. Often, in dreams, as with myths and folk-tales, protagonists find themselves lost in a strange, dark, enchanted forest. Probing one's unconscious, which is what we must do in order to interpret most dreams, can sometimes be like entering a deep, mysterious forest filled with unforeseen phenomenon – the hiding place of your darkest fears and deepest desires. It requires some courage to traverse these shadowy, uncharted realms of one's inner self. Be prepared for the unexpected, but be fearless. Remember that you are safe and inviolable in your own world of dreams.

OVERLOOKING THE OBVIOUS

There is another concern to be aware of when analyzing your own dreams. Many years ago, when I worked as an editor for a monthly magazine, it was standard practice to have a copy-editor, other than the author of a given article, doing a final edit and proof-read. The reason for this was simple – we knew from experience that writers would habitually skip over their own mistakes, when editing their own work. A similar phenomenon can be seen with self-interpretation of dreams. It's easy to miss or dismiss elements, in our own dreams, that might be obvious to a therapist or another person with whom you share the dream. Be diligent to include every recalled detail about a dream, when relating your dream, or writing it down. Like the writer editing their own work, this can be tricky. It requires considerable, mental discipline to avoid overlooking or ignoring significant elements, hiding in plain sight, in your own dreams.

With dreams the possibility of misinterpretation goes beyond merely overlooking obvious details. Freud addressed this major challenge to cogent dream interpretation, which he called ***"resistance"***. His patients had a tendency to overlook crucial details in their dreams, and to distort the dream narrative in the retelling. It remains one of the therapist's primary functions, to keep their patient on track; recognizing that, often, the really crucial symbols in a dream are the very ones the dreamer overlooks or resists. It is consistently these very details, seemingly insignificant and irrelevant, that are crucial keys to understanding the meaning of a dream. When working without the assistance of a therapist, it is critical to pay extra close attention to details that might, at first glance, appear totally absurd or unimportant. Because of ego-resistance, such details are often hot-spots of meaning.

DON'T GET STUCK

Sometimes, a specific dream or dream detail will fizzle out of consciousness, leaving a mere ripple of memory in its wake. Most of us have had the rather annoying experience of temporarily forgetting something, like the name of a person or place, something that we know that we know. The escaped memory irks us, hovering tantalizingly, just behind the curtain of consciousness. The harder we try to recapture this memory the more it eludes us. Suddenly, minutes, hours or days after we have given up seeking this memory, seemingly out of nowhere, the memory comes back as clear as crystal.

This type of delinquent, dream detail can really slow down the interpretation process. When a dream detail escapes, in the midst of the recall process, I have one simple rule to avoid getting mired down:

IF YOU CAN'T REMEMBER, FORGET ABOUT IT!!!

Chances are it will come back to you when you least expect it.

STEP BY STEP GUIDE
TO INTERPRETING YOUR OWN DREAMS

Below you will find a series of steps that I have developed and been using to successfully interpret dreams for over thirty years. I'm confident that working with these steps will get you started on a valuable path to interpreting your own dreams. These steps should not be viewed as a meticulous formula that will yield a predictable outcome. They are simply laid-out as a guide, and the user should feel free to follow any roads that might open up along the way.

The method and process of interpreting a dream varies from dream to dream. Sometimes the meaning and significance of a dream presents itself clearly with very little need for interpretation or decoding. More often, it is like detective work, gathering clues, looking for patterns and piecing together a puzzle of extremely complex ideas and emotions. The *"aha"* moment, when the dream's primary message is understood, may come at any time in the process. Often, interpreting a single, symbolic element will swiftly provide a key for understanding an entire dream.

The interpretation process is distinctive for each dream. Follow the clues and your hunches down whatever rabbit holes they may lead. If, at last, the dream remains a puzzle, try sleeping on it.

STEP ONE

START BY RECORDING THE DREAM

It's a good idea to write down or record a dream, as soon as possible, after awakening from the dream, before the details become murky or disappear into the unconscious like a shooting star in the night sky. Often a dream memory will evaporate within seconds of awakening. Sometimes a faint image, a word, a song, a taste are all that remain.

A vivid dream-memory may surface or resurface, anytime after the dream actually occurred. There are those visions that continue to vanish and re-emerge, again and again, over many years, even throughout a lifetime. Whenever the dream memory is clear, write it down. Don't hesitate; it may disappear a moment later.

In relating the dream, start off in the present perfect tense then go to regular present tense. Staying in the present tense, makes the dream easier to visualize and narrate – For example consider this brief dream of mine:

"I am walking down a shady, cobblestone street. (present-perfect = I **am** walking). *I am looking at my shoes; they are made of embroidered silk* (continue and stay in the present tense). *I am in an old-time village. It looks like somewhere in southern Europe, but I have no conception of an actual, geographic location. I look up and see a stone*

castle off in the misty distance. Suddenly it starts to rain heavily. I see a sign swinging in the wind and rain outside an antique shop. I try, but I can't read the writing on the sign. I run into the shop to get out of the rain. A jingly bell rings as I close the door behind me. When I get inside the shop I realize I am at some sort of bazaar, with a variety of items on display. There are books, exotic fabrics, musical instruments and antique furnishings available. Soft music is coming from a room at the back of the shop. I enter this room to find a gathering of lovely, formally dressed women who all have deep-purple hair. The women all carry parasols. They all sing sweetly as they walk to and fro, encircling me. Suddenly I find myself in the middle of a forest. The women have transformed into trees and they continue singing. It's a lovely, wordless, melancholy song that I faintly recognize from the past."

I awoke at this point. The melody of the tree song stayed with me, for a few moments, but soon is forgotten. Upon awakening, I recalled the dream quite vividly and jotted it down in a notebook that I keep by my bedside. Once I had written down the dream, I was able to re-visualize it clearly, in my mind's eye, just by reading my rough, point-form narrative.

On the surface, dreams, like the one above, often do not provide a logical sequence of events. The dreamer might find themselves inexplicably transported from one setting to another. Events may occur, seemingly, out of sequence or several events may occur simultaneously. Weird as the dream narrative might seem, when recording, we must try to stick to the raw, bare-bones memory, without any reordering or embellishment. When relating our dreams there is a strong inclination to impose conscious additions, in order to make the narrative more comfortably logical. Often, it requires psychological discipline to avoid imposing such rearrangements onto your dream. However, the inclination to embellish, edit or rewrite our dreams can, in itself, provide clues about the meaning of the dream. If you recognize a part of your dream that you are disposed to change or fix because it somehow makes you uncomfortable, or it just doesn't seem right, then it's a good bet that there is an important clue, a hot spot, right there. The incongruent, illogical, awkward components, in your dreams, are the very ones that will regularly open doors of deeper meaning.

To summarize: When writing down your dream narrative, use the present tense, keep to a simple, conversational tone and include as many details as you can recall. Avoid the tendency to impose an editorial structure onto the dream, even when the dream-play appears to be nonsensical or bizarre. Pay special attention to those parts of the dream that you have the impulse to change or ignore. Once you've recorded your dream, read it over and assign a quick title.

You can format your notebook as next: 

<table>
<tr><td>Date</td><td>Dreamer's Name</td><td>Dream's Working Title</td></tr>
<tr><td></td><td></td><td></td></tr>
</table>

Your Dream Narrative

Describe the dream in story form, in present tense. Include as many details as you can recall. Avoid the tendency to impose an editorial structure onto the dream, even when the dream play appears to be nonsensical or bizarre. Use as much space as you need. . .

STEP TWO

ANSWER BASIC QUESTIONS ABOUT THE DREAM

After you've written down your dream, read it to yourself, preferably out loud. Now step back and ask five, pivotal questions. Jot down the answers in your notepad. Concise, short forms will do here.

<table>
<tr>
<td>

1) **What is the locale or setting of the dream? Note your location at the very beginning of the dream and as it changes throughout. Does the dream feel like past present or future (it may be all three).**

</td>
<td>

Begin with generalities: Are you in a familiar place or a strange place, or one that is strangely familiar? As you proceed, get more specific with descriptive details: Are you in a futuristic city; upon a lofty mountain top; in a dark, mysterious forest; in a big, wooden house with many rooms; etcetera, etcetera? Note a sequence of changing settings.

</td>
</tr>
</table>

| **2)** What is the mood of the dream at the very beginning? How does the mood of the dream change throughout? | Is there a dominating emotion(s) that pervades the dream? What is the atmosphere – i.e. joyful, gloomy, bright, foggy, tempestuous, peaceful, strange, familiar etc? How do emotions transform throughout the dream? As with pathetic fallacy in literature, weather conditions, i.e. calm or stormy, will be an indicator of the general mood surrounding the dream. Does the dream feel like past, present or future? It may be all three. |

3) Who are you in the dream? What are you feeling? Your perspective and your persona.	Sometimes you are solely an observer with no active role in a dream. Other times you may be fully immersed in the dream. Also, you may, at once, be observer and participant in your dream. What is your persona? How do you see yourself in this dream, if at all — your approximate age, your costume, your role, your general condition? Do you have intent in the dream? Perhaps you are on a journey, trying to find something or someone? What are your feelings in the dream; lonely, excited, fearful, calm, weak, powerful, etc, etc?

4) What are the main actions and activities in the dream?	*Exploring actions and activities in dreams is crucial for interpretation. Actions are usually the most consistent, symbolic elements in a dream; meaning they are very closely related in both their latent and manifest aspects. See step four. Follow the action.*
5) What is the highlight or the most intense moment(s) in the dream?	*Note the pivotal moment or moments in the dream.*

STEP THREE

FIRST IMPRESSIONS: DO A PRELIMINARY INTERPRETATION

Although an instant interpretation is not uncommon, most often the meaning of a dream remains, vague or unclear upon the first reading. Usually, at this point, the dream remains largely incomprehensible, in which case you can move on to the next steps. As we proceed to the next steps, we use associative techniques to explore specific elements of a dream. By analyzing the individual symbols from the dream narrative, we discern repetitive motifs and patterns that guide us towards a multi-layered interpretation.

However, sometimes, a clear and direct interpretation of the dream offers itself up with the first hearing. Re-read your dream description and review your answers to the five, preliminary questions above. Without further analyzing specific elements, write down, **in one sentence** what you think the general theme of the dream is about. The essential meaning of the dream may begin to reveal itself to the dreamer, at this early point. Like a proverbial light-bulb turning on, the dreamer immediately connects aspects of the dream to their current, life experiences.

If you do feel, at this early point, that you understand the core meaning of your dream, it's a good idea to promptly write down your essential understanding of the dream in several, short sentences. Verbalizing your understanding, in a concise statement, will help you to preserve the clarity of the moment, which very often dissipates like a wisp of smoke in the breeze. Even if you feel you've grasped the primary meaning of a dream, don't stop with your preliminary interpretation. Remember that a single dream symbol may have multiple meanings, and likewise a single dream might have several, forceful layers of meaning. If you do have a strong preliminary interpretation, then use it as a compass as you dig deeper into the dream, but stay open to the possibility that new, unexpected meanings could arise independently of your preliminary interpretation.

STEP FOUR

REVIEW, IDENTIFY AND FOLLOW THE ACTION

Follow the action. Exploring actions and activities in dreams is crucial for interpretation. Actions are usually the most consistent, symbolic elements in a dream; meaning they are very closely related in both their latent and manifest aspects. In the next step we will analyze particular elements in the dream. Once we discover the symbolic meaning of an element we can substitute the symbol's latent meaning onto the line of action. For example: Someone dreams of "***a clown walking blindly off a precipitous cliff but landing safely in a patch of soft grass below***". The clown may hold a range of symbolic significance for the dreamer, as might the cliff and the grass below; but the action, of walking off a cliff and landing safely, retains its obvious, idiomatic meaning. Let's say that, after analyzing the clown element in the dream, the dreamer has uncovered that the clown symbolizes themselves in a new, romantic relationship that they are entering. If the dreamer substitutes their self, instead of the clown, into the line of action, they may now read the dream: ***"When it comes to my new, romantic relationship I am walking off a cliff (stepping blindly into the unknown) and hoping that I'll somehow land safely."*** The line of action in the dream remains essentially unchanged, even when the rest of the dream elements have been symbolically transformed.

STEP FIVE
IDENTIFY AND PROFILE KEY ELEMENTS

Once you've recorded and reviewed the dream, answered the general questions, attempted a preliminary interpretation and followed a line of action, begin the process of identifying and profiling the key, dream elements. The dream elements include each of the characters, places and things that appear within a dream. To start, you can create a list of all the dream elements by simply writing down significant nouns from the initial dream record. Once you've created your list, beginning with the elements that seem most central to the dream narrative, you may create profiles using the charts provided on the next pages. Exploring the ins and outs, of a primary element, typically brings some revealing, symbolic correlations to the surface. Often you will discover unexpected, intersecting touch-points with more than one element. Once you've explored one major element, you can go on to profile others.

Begin by using the charts, on the following pages, to profile a person, animal or thing in your dream. Then go on to analyze these dream elements with Free, and then Direct Association techniques. You can do a profile for each of the elements in a particular dream, but it's best to start with just a few of the most prominent characters or things. (See sample pages next chapter)

Chart One on the next page provides a handy format to record a descriptive profile of a specific element:

CHART ONE	DESCRIPTIVE PROFILE OF A DREAM ELEMENT(person, animal or thing)
ELEMENT'S NAME, IDENTITY, DESIGNATION (known or unknown?)	*If you do not know the name or designation, use a very brief description. i.e.; 'Little, Golden-Haired Girl.'*
GENERAL DESCRIPTION, AGE, APPEARANCE, CLOTHING, UNUSUAL FEATURES, ACCOMPANYING OBJECTS	
PRIMARY ACTIONS AND OR SPEECH	
DREAMER'S IMMEDIATE, GUT RESPONSE TO THIS ELEMENT	

STEP SIX

FREE ASSOCIATE ON THE ELEMENTS

As we have seen, **Free Association** is the process of noting the first thing that comes to mind, when presented with a specific, dream element. The method is simple, but often not easy because our conscious ego-mind must suspend its natural inclination to censor and reorder. It's important to record an immediate response, even if it seems inappropriate, nonsensical or silly.

When Free Associating dream elements, one should respond to a particular element precisely as it appears in the dream. For example: You dream of an apple. Was it big or small? Was it succulent or shriveled, etc.etc? Be descriptive when introducing a dream element for association, but don't go overboard. At this point, keep the element's description concise, using not more than two or three adjectives. An exception is when an association is built around a specific memory of a particular event or experience, which might require a few more words to characterize.

Free Association is typically done in three steps. For example: The element from one of my dreams is a ***tart, juicy apple***. What is the first thing that pops into my mind when I think of a tart, juicy apple? My first association was the ***i) Disney movie Snow White*** (this is the first movie I can recall seeing). **ii)** My immediate association with Snow White was a particular, early, ***childhood memory of being frightened and fascinated in a dark movie theatre.***

iii) My instantaneous association to being in a dark movie theater was the ***smell of buttered popcorn***. The key, to using the free-association method successfully, is non-interference. Resisting the impulse to change, censor or ignore your instantaneous associations, requires some mental discipline and, sometimes, even courage. However, it is crucial to acknowledge the immediate, unobstructed image, that pops into your mind and to record it, no matter how silly, or inappropriate it may seem.

Remember, as often as not, the associative sequence will appear, at least at first glance, to be devoid of any logic. Your free association might well have unfolded in a seemingly irrational manner. Just as dreams may appear to be irrational, so too a series of free associations may also seem to defy logic. But, make no mistake; free associations are not random. In fact they are among our best interpretive tools because, ideally, they emerge, uncensored, directly from the unconscious.

At this point our free associations appear, by and large, arbitrary and irrational, like the scattered pieces of a mystery puzzle, but as we proceed, with our interpretation, these scattered pieces are reassembled into a meaningful picture. As you record and review your free associations, definite patterns will soon emerge. In the next step we will work with Direct Associations which, unlike Free Associations, provide a more deliberate, thought-out, analysis of what dream elements symbolize to the dreamer. You will likely discover that your Free Associations and your Direct Associations have some motifs in common. These are hotspots that usually point to something of extra significance.

Note the first, spontaneous answer that comes to mind.

CHART TWO 3-LEVEL FREE-ASSOCIATIONS ON A DREAM ELEMENT	
NAME /DESIGNATION OF ELEMENT:	
STEPS	**DREAMERS IMMEDIATE RESPONSE**
i) Picture the image of the person, animal or thing as they appeared in the dream, and then give your immediate, first response.	i)
ii) Free associate on your first response	ii)
iii) Free associate on your second response	iii)

STEP SEVEN

DIRECT ASSOCIATIONS

Working with the previously identified, dream elements, we can now go on to analyze, more comprehensively, the symbolic meanings that each element might hold for the dreamer. At this point the psychoanalytic process really begins. We begin to investigate the dream in analytic terms, consciously unfolding layers of interpretation and cogently linking up ideas. In its very early days psychoanalysis was often referred to as the *"talking cure"*. And this is just what is required at this stage of the interpretive process. Talk, to your guide, or to yourself, or write down your thoughts about the elements that occurred in the dream and consciously explore them. Take special note when you find that your direct associations match up with your previous free associations. Remember, when exploring direct associations of a dream element, a person, animal or thing will often carry multiple meanings. Often a symbol will represent more than one quality or a combination of qualities.

---

1) A person, animal or thing might **represent a specific aspect, quality or character trait of the dreamer.** A dream symbol could represent the dreamer's ego, superego, id, libido, shadow-self, self-doubt, creative muse, anima/animus, talent, addiction, sense of humor, specific hope or fear, etc. etc. An element could also represent courage, or paranoia, wisdom or foolishness, sensuality or frigidity, impetuousness or carefulness, reminiscence or forgetfulness, loyalty or faithlessness, etc. etc.

---

2) A person, animal or thing might **represent a relationship or a type of relationship** like parent, spouse, sibling, friend, enemy, etc.

3) A person, animal or thing may **represent an idea or an emotion, or several ideas and emotions simultaneously**. Given the multi-layered nature of dream symbols, analysis will often indicate a poetically crafted representation of highly complex emotions and ideas.

4) A person, animal or thing might **represent a specific activity or event in a particular time and place.** For example: one might associate a spotted pony with the first time one attended a carnival.

5) A person, animal or thing may **replace or represent another person animal or thing.** You may dream about your friend Mary but Mary is really Sue. Mary and Sue may be associated for a wide variety of reasons including similar appearance, similar relationship, similar attitudes etc. etc.

6) A person, animal or thing appearing in a dream may simply **represent themselves or an aspect of themselves** in the dream.

You can set up a chart, like the one on the next page, to record Direct Associations on a Dream Element (conscious, symbolic associations that the element holds for the dreamer).

<table>
<tr><td>DIRECT ASSOCIATIONS</td><td>ELEMENT'S NAME:</td></tr>
<tr><td>

Your **immediate emotional response** to the appearance of a person, animal or thing in your dream.

Ask – How do I feel about this element during the dream? Do my feelings towards this element change throughout the dream?

</td><td></td></tr>
<tr><td>

This person, animal or thing might represent **an aspect of your personality or psyche.**

Ask – What quality or character trait of myself do I associate with the dream element?

</td><td></td></tr>
<tr><td>

This person, animal or thing might represent **a relationship** itself **or a type of relationship**.

Ask – What is my essential relationship (if any) with this person animal or thing? What is my role in the relationship? What is this person's, animal's or thing's role

</td><td></td></tr>
</table>

A person, animal or thing may **represent an idea or an emotion, or several ideas and emotions simultaneously**. **Ask** – Does this element represent a universal concept or emotion?	
The person, animal or thing might represent a **specific activity, or event, or a specific time and place.** **Ask** – In the context of this dream does this person animal or thing connect to a specific time or event in my life?	
A person, animal or thing may **replace or represent another person, animal or thing.** **Ask** – Is this element strongly associated with another person animal or thing - bread and butter.	
A person, animal or thing may simply **represent themselves in the dream.** Note any qualifications as to age, appearance, demeanor etc. that might appear out of the ordinary. **Ask** – What is different about the person as you know them in waking life and as they appear in the dream? Differences are flashpoints of meaning.	

STEP EIGHT (Optional)
ROLE-PLAYING DREAM ELEMENTS

I've included role-playing as an optional step for those who are comfortable with acting-out, and this may not be for everyone. The basic technique is to identify and vocalize with a dream element, like a method actor who actualizes the real emotions of a character. The dreamer might choose one or several, significant elements to verbally act out. The elements may include any characters or things from the dream. This method is really a combination of free association and direct association techniques, whereby one takes the time to articulate an immediate impression. Like Free Association, Role-Playing seeks to make direct contact with the unconscious. Like Direct Association, this method requires some reflective analysis of the element.

Role-playing of dream elements was popularized by prominent, psychotherapist Fredrick Perls (1893 –1970) as a key component of his Gestalt therapeutic approach. The premise, of Gestalt dream therapy, is that every element in a dream is actually an aspect of the dreamer. He views dreams as ***"an existential experience created by, and of, and for the dreamer"*** (Perls, F. S. (1969). Gestalt Therapy Verbatim). The goal of Gestalt therapy is to reclaim disowned or impoverished aspects of ourselves and reintegrate them into our whole personality.

The basic operands, of this exercise, is to first identify elements in a dream, and then to identify with and verbally role-play individual elements. This is possible and relevant simply because every element, in a dream, is created by the dreamer out of their own psyche. Role playing, like dream description, is best done in the present tense, meaning one should describe or act-out their dreams, as if they were occurring in the moment. For example, suppose you dream of walking through a house with many rooms and discovering different elements in each room. The dreamer could begin by identifying with the whole house – *"I am this house!"* Like a method actor, seek the essence of the object, creature or person you are identifying with. How does this house feel? Is it old or young or ageless? Is it sad or happy or filled with mixed emotions? Once you have explored your identification with the house you can move on to role-play the other elements of the dream. If you dreamt of sitting in chair – become the chair for a moment and then speak as the chair. If you swam in a lake – become the lake and then say what you are feeling, describe yourself; *"I am a lake full of water. My water is clean and pure etc. etc."*

This method, of identification and verbalizing dream elements, generally taps into a rich mine of meaningful associations. It is helpful to have a trusted, dream guide when working with the Gestalt technique. An experienced guide can direct the dreamer, and serve as an audience that the dreamer can play to when acting-out a dream element. A dream guide may also write down significant details to discuss later. However your guide should be someone you are fully comfortable with, in order to avoid inhibiting your experience.

With or without a guide, when one allows oneself to identify with and inhabit a dream element, the gut- level reactions will, most likely, not be forgotten. You should come out of this exercise with a more visceral understanding of your dream.

STEP NINE
LOOKING FOR PATTERNS, MAKING CONNECTIONS

Chances are, at this point, that you've already got a basic understanding of your dream, just by having done some of the association exercises. After compiling your charts and notes, consider all the clues that you now have in front of you. Follow up on your hunches, using the charts as your data base of clues. You can write on the charts and draw connecting lines between clues that you feel are related. Circle repeated motifs. It is helpful to have a notepad in which you can jot down, in point form, your thoughts as they develop.

A good starting point is to compare your free associations to your direct associations. It is highly significant when the same idea surfaces in both your free associations and your direct associations. Note concurrent patterns as they emerge? Do some of the elements, in your dream, and their associations seem to point to similar ideas? Are ideas or themes repeated throughout the dream? Ideas that are repeated, in various symbolic forms within a dream, are usually the most proliferate. By meditating on and discussing the repeated themes that emerge from a dream, a coherent sequence, which speaks to the inner life of the dreamer, will ultimately emerge. Once you've unravelled the threads of meaning, begin to tie them together. See an example in the next pages.

WORKING WITH A DREAM
EXAMPLE OF A STEP BY STEP DREAM ANALYSIS
USING THE DREAM-SELFIE CHARTS

Below you will find an abridged example of how to use the charts to get clues and unravel the meaning of a dream. I've used an actual dream with the permission of the dreamer. All names have been changed. The subject is a male, age 36 at the time of the dream. Note: this is a condensed version of the analysis; the actual process was more extensive and included in-depth analysis of several elements from the dream.

STEP ONE – RECORD THE DREAM

<table>
<tr><td colspan="2">Dreamer: John (alias), Male, 36 years old at time of dream.</td></tr>
<tr><td>Title: "Two Sisters"</td><td>Date:
010101</td></tr>
<tr><td colspan="2">Descriptive Narrative – (present tense). Use additional pages as required.
John: I am standing, with some vaguely familiar but unidentified, young people, in the back alley behind my high school. My older brother Jed appears, wearing a green Robin-hood style cap</td></tr>
</table>

and a brightly coloured, sports jacket with writing on the back. I can see the writing clearly but, weirdly, I can't read it. Jed is riding a huge, scruffy, two-humped camel through the back alley behind the schoolyard. He rides the camel around the school yard a couple of times, waving and smiling at me and the other kids in the school yard. He seems to be having a good time. He doesn't say anything. Suddenly, the camel starts to walk backwards. Jed looks silly. I feel embarrassed. Silently my brother rides off backwards across the school field and disappears beyond the horizon. Imperceptibly the crowd has dispersed. All of the other people have left the scene now. Two pretty young girls approach me, from the alley way, walking arm in arm. I feel that I know them, but can't name them. They look similar, like sisters, but one is a little taller. The sisters are both very good-looking, with the same shade of radiant golden hair. The smaller one has an enticing, artful expression. The taller girl seems naïve, innocent and inexperienced. I am attracted to them both. They tell me I must choose between one or the other, but I cannot have them both. The girls never speak individually — when the two girls speak, they speak together in unison. I try to make a deal with them because I feel they should stay together — actually I cannot see how they can be parted because their arms are linked tightly together like a pretzel. It seems like a catch 22 situation and I feel confused and frustrated. Suddenly the scene changes and I am, by myself, on a lonely road in open country. In the distance, walking off towards the far off hills, I see the two sisters, still arm and arm but now they are the same height. I watch them wistfully as they drift off towards the horizon — and here the dream ends.

*   *   *

STEP TWO – PRELIMINARY QUESTIONS

What is the locale or setting of the dream? Note your location at the very beginning of the dream and as it changes throughout. Does the dream feel like past, present or future? (It may be all three)

John: i) My high school yard. ii) On a dusty, lonely road in open country in some unknown land.

What is the mood(s) of the dream? Especially how did you feel at the very beginning and the very end of the dream?

John: The mood changed from levity, to envy, to annoyance, to embarrassment, to eroticism, to confusion to indecision to a sense of loss to a feeling of moving on.

Who are you in the dream? Your perspective and your persona. What are you feeling?

John: I am myself but I am younger, still a high school student. I recall now that I was carrying a textbook and a notebook in the first part of the dream. I had forgotten this detail. I'm like a young student in this dream, learning about life. I don't know how I dressed or looked but felt like my younger self. I feel I am looking back at the past, but it also feels like the present. At the end of the dream, as I look at the two sisters in the distance, I feel I'm gazing at a distant, indefinite future.

What are the main actions and activities occurring in the dream? Especially what are your actions?

John: *At first, I am mainly an observer rather than a participant, although I am immersed in the dream. I am standing and watching. I don't do much. Mostly just watching my brother's antics. Strangely, I can't read the writing on the back of his jacket. He is riding a camel, waving and smiling at me and the other kids. He doesn't speak. Suddenly the camel walks backwards and disappears into the distance. A little latter I interact with the two sisters, who walk towards me and stand, as if waiting, in front of me. I begin talking to them. Trying to work something out. The girls never speak individually – when the two girls speak, they speak together in unison. I am feeling frustrated, but suddenly, the conversation stops and I am transported to a lofty locale removed from the two sisters, but I can still see them walking off together in the distance. At the end of the dream I am walking slowly, while I watch the two sisters disappear. My walking feels more like floating. I feel elevated but with a sense of sadness and loss.*

STEP THREE

FIRST IMPRESSIONS: PRELIMINARY INTERPRETATION

Re-read your dream description and review your answers to the preliminary questions above. Without further analyzing specific elements, write down, in one sentence, what you think the dream is about. The essential meaning of the dream may begin to reveal itself, to the dreamer, at this early point, but often the dream remains largely incomprehensible, in which case **you can move on to the next step.**

John: *At this point my dream seems bizarre and nonsensical to me. I have an inkling that it might have something to do with my relationship to my brother. The two sisters in the dream vaguely remind me of girls from my teenage years, but I don't understand their significance or why they are together.*

STEP FOUR – REVIEW, IDENTIFY AND FOLLOW THE ACTION

John: *My main actions as they unfold in this dream are: standing –watching – feeling amused and then embarrassed – feeling attraction to two girls – trying to make a deal– feeling frustrated – feeling bewildered – slowly walking alone– watching and contemplating – feeling melancholy but vaguely uplifted and hopeful.*

STEP FIVE – LOOKING AT INDIVIDUAL ELEMENTS

John's Dream, which he called "<u>The Two Sisters</u>", had a number of elements, each of which we explored individually. Here are the charts that John filled out regarding the appearance of his brother Jed in this dream. John's brother was an important element in this dream, representing multiple facets of John himself.

<table>
<tr><td>CHART ONE :
DESCRIPTIVE PROFILE OF A DREAM ELEMENT</td></tr>
<tr><td>DREAM TITLE : The Two Sisters</td></tr>
<tr><td>ELEMENT'S NAME OR DESIGNATION:
My older brother Jed.</td></tr>
<tr><td>GENERAL DESCRIPTION:
APPARENT AGE, CLOTHING, APPEARANCE, ACCOMPANYING OBJECTS,UNUSUAL FEATURES</td></tr>
<tr><td>John: My brother Jed is riding a big, shaggy camel. Jed appears wearing a green Robin hood style cap and his high school sports-jacket. As kids Jed and I</td></tr>
</table>

enjoyed watching Robin Hood on television together. This gave me the feeling that I was dealing with some issue rooted in the past. The Robin Hood cap suggested the ideas of light-hearted thievery, and also conveyed a feeling of swaggering, adolescent bravado. In waking life my brother Jed is 39 but he appeared to be only a teenager in the dream. I understood this to mean that the dream was rooted in the past in his and my own teenage years.

ELEMENT'S PRIMARY ACTIONS OR SPEECH

John: Jed rides the camel around the school yard a couple of times and waves and smiles to me and the other kids in the school yard. He seems to be having a good time. He doesn't say anything. Suddenly the camel starts to walk backwards. Jed looks silly.

<table>
<tr><td>

DREAMER'S EMOTIONAL RESPONSE TO THIS ELEMENT

</td></tr>
<tr><td>

John: *An emotional mixture of amusement, embarrassment, annoyance, allegiance and fear. As a kid, I would often have these feelings as Jed's younger brother. At first I felt pride that Jed was my brother because he seemed popular with the crowd riding around on his camel, but when he loses control of the camel I feel embarrassed.*

</td></tr>
</table>

STEP SIX

FREE ASSOCIATION ON A DREAM ELEMENT

In the next step John proceeded to Free Associate on his brother Jed as he appeared in the dream. As we have seen, **Free Association** is the process of noting the first thing that comes to mind, when presented with a specific, dream element. Free Association is typically done in three steps. All three of John's instantaneous responses were closely associated with childhood and adolescent memories. John's free associations appear on the following page.

3 LEVEL FREE ASSOCIATION ON A DREAM ELEMENT

Note the first, spontaneous answer that comes to mind.

CHART TWO THREE LEVEL FREE ASSOCIATION ON A DREAM ELEMENT	NAME / DESIGNATION OF ELEMENT: *Jed (my brother)*
STEPS	**FREE ASSOCIATION**
i) Picture the image of the person, animal or thing as they appeared in the dream and then give your <u>immediate</u>, first response.	**John:** *i) My immediate association to the appearance of my brother Jed, in the dream: <u>a rodeo clown</u>*
ii) Free Associate on your first response.	*ii) My immediate association to a rodeo clown: <u>clown drinking whiskey backstage</u> (this image of the clown drinking backstage is based on an actual childhood memory)*
iii) Free Associate on the secondary response.	*iii) My immediate association to drinking whiskey backstage: <u>smoking behind the school</u> (both represented risky and potentially dangerous behavior).*

STEP SEVEN

DIRECT ASSOCIATIONS ON A DREAM ELEMENT

We continued to focus on John's brother Jed with direct associations, consciously developing analytical meanings that the symbol holds for the dreamer.

CHART THREE DIRECT ASSOCIATIONS	ELEMENT'S NAME: My Brother Jed
Your **immediate emotional response** to the appearance of a person, animal or thing in your dream. __Ask__ – How do I feel about this element during the dream? Do my feelings towards this element change throughout the dream?	**John:** It feels like I'm back in my high-school days. Students used to hang-out in a hidden alley just behind the schoolyard, smoking cigarettes. A lot of social interaction occurred there in that secreted alley.
This person, animal or thing might represent **an aspect of your personality or psyche.** __Ask__ – What quality or character trait of myself do I associate with the dream element?	**John:** In waking life my brother is competitive and but he's a straight shooter and rarely underhanded. He's not a person that will try to bend the rules to win attention, but in my dream I perceive him as being mischievous and devious. More like me I guess.

This person, animal or thing might represent **a relationship** itself **or a type of relationship**.

<u>Ask</u> – What is my essential relationship (if any) with this person animal or thing? What is my role in the relationship? What is this person's, animal's or thing's role?

A person, animal or thing may **represent an idea or an emotion, or several ideas and emotions simultaneously**.

<u>Ask</u> – Does this element represent a universal concept or emotion?

The person, animal or thing might represent a **specific activity, or event, or a specific time and place.** **Ask** – In the context of this dream does this person animal or thing connect to a specific time or event in my life?	**John:** *High-school days*
A person, animal or thing may **replace or represent another person animal or thing.** **Ask** – How Does this element share similar appearance or other qualities that suggest it is replacing something or someone else?	**John:** *I feel Jed is representing me.*
A person, animal or thing may simply **represent themselves in the dream.** Note any qualifications as to age, appearance, demeanor etc. that might appear out of the ordinary. **Ask** – What is different about the person as you know them in waking life and as they appear in the dream? Differences are flash-points of meaning.	**John:** *Jed's behavior in the dream is very different from his waking demeanor. In the dream he doesn't seem to recognize me or try to communicate with me. This makes me suspect that it's not really my brother I'm dreaming about.*

STEP EIGHT: (Optional)

ROLE-PLAYING DREAM ELEMENT

Although John was not comfortable trying to verbally identify with a dream element (too dramatic and emotionally intense), he did attempt it with one element—the brightly coloured, sports jacket that Jed was wearing as he rode around on the camel in John's dream.

John speaking as the sports, jacket: " *I am a colourful, team jacket. I want to show that I am young and strong. I am a super star and I want to show it, but people don't seem to recognize my potential. I want to display my colours and get noticed. I should be seen in the spotlight, and be worn by a heroic, team leader; but I don't know which team and nobody seems to notice me.*"

John's dramatic-identification exercise, with the sports jacket, was one of the most poignant moments in the interpretation process. When he reviewed what he had verbalized, when speaking as the jacket, John was surprised to uncover an aspect of his personality which had previously remained concealed. While viewing himself as highly independent and with little need of attention from others, John clearly recognized his own hidden, egotistical view of himself and his desire for ego-boosting attention. In the next step John uncovers many more aspects of his inner life that had previously lay hidden in his unconscious.

STEP NINE

LOOKING FOR PATTERNS, MAKING CONNECTIONS DECIPHERING AND ANALYZING JOHN'S DREAM

Although it was not particularly lengthy, the 'Two Sisters' dream proved to be a rich mine of profound, personal significance for John. We can see, from the above examples on John's charts, that profiling and interpreting even one character or element can lead towards multiple layers of meaning within the dream. More so, after profiling multiple elements, specific, repeated themes and motifs will emerge. These recurring themes and motifs usually point towards highly meaningful interpretations.

Initially John and I spent several sessions (approximately four hours in total) working on this one dream. We analyzed the main characters and their actions. The dream proved to be a deep well of imagery that spoke to some of John's core issues, and it became a constant reference point on his personal journey of self-discovery.

Here is a glimpse at how some of John's dream analysis unfolded:

The topic of smoking cigarettes kept popping up on John's dream charts. The element, that John began his free associations with, was the camel that his brother was riding in the dream. His first, free association on the camel, was with Camel Brand cigarettes. John recalled that his father smoked this filter-less brand, and that his own first, nicotine puffs were pilfered from his father's pack. He associated the whole scene with his youth in high school, when he started smoking with his friends in the alley beside the school. Ironically it was John who tried smoking first, and then dared his older brother to try. The dream provided much insight for John about his relationship with his brother Jed but, even more so, about himself and his own interactions with others.

In the dream, his brother Jed symbolized John's young ego motivations for smoking – trying to look cool and mature, and seeking attention. John recognized instantly that he was seeing himself in his brother. He realized how silly he must have looked smoking back then, *"like a drunken clown"*. Shortly after high-school Jed quit smoking, but, at the time of the dream 15 years later, John was still struggling with a nicotine addiction. In addition to his tobacco addiction, John had taken to alcohol use during his college days, and this also continued to be an ongoing issue. At the time of the dream he was drinking almost every night. The dream showed that John had a double-addiction, symbolized by the two sisters in his dream.

The two sisters who appeared in the dream were obviously linked together. They also revealed multiple layers of meaning. When we analyzed them, as a single element, it became clear that these two sisters represented, on one level, John's nicotine and alcohol addictions. The slightly younger sister represented alcohol because this addiction was introduced a little more recently in John's life. With some further analysis, John realized that his use of alcohol was linked to smoking tobacco, and that his nicotine and alcohol addictions were correlated and interdependent. When he drank he smoked, and when he smoked he drank. He also realized that to break one of the addictions he would have to break both.

Upon further analyzing all the elements in the dream John realized that he had other, deep-rooted motivations for smoking and drinking that pointed towards his sense of competitiveness and self-worth. The green Robin Hood style cap that Jed wore in the dream turned out to have a direct association with John's father who used to wear a green fedora. Their father was, hypocritically, quite judgemental of John and, at the same time, showed partiality to his brother Jed. His father projected his own failings onto John and his aspirations onto Jed. As a result John, who identified with his father, developed a deep-seated and mostly unconscious feeling of inferiority. This discovery opened a whole, alternative avenue of inquiry for this dream. John's unconscious feelings of resentment and inadequacy, in addition to feeding his addictions, overflowed into all aspects of his life including work, family and social bonding. It was all connected – his addictions, his sense of low self-worth and his relationships with others.

Armed with this self-knowledge and a strong determination to heal his addictive behaviours, John courageously set himself on a path to breaking both his nicotine and alcohol addictions, and this he did within six months of having this dream. Resolving the inner conflict, created by John's nicotine/alcohol addictions, turned out to be just one of several, primary messages gleaned from this dream. Through the magic mirror of his dream, John was able to see what his own motivations for smoking and drinking had been, and how his show-off behaviour was often compensation for a deep-seated insecurity.

But there was a lot more to come. The two sisters, as well as other elements in the dream, had layers of meaning that related to John's core motivations and relationships. The dream provided a prototype, which recreated an elemental situation, enjoining John's primary, decision-making process. When John worked on his free and direct associations, he discovered that the two sisters, in addition to representing John's double addiction, were also associated with two actual, young women whom he had known in high school, although they were not really sisters. They were friends and both had the same chestnut-coloured hair. One of the girls was in the grade behind him, the other in the grade ahead. John had even dated the younger girl, who really liked him and became an easy conquest on his teenage, make-out list. But secretly he longed for the older girl, who remained unattainable and aloof. The older sister was the prize that his heart truly longed for, but she remained always beyond his reach. His longing for the implausible, led John to devalue and even spurn his real relationship with the younger sister. John recognized, after searching into this dream, that he had the very common human disposition of chasing after and longing for the unattainable, while taking for granted life's, manifest endowments. He realized that he had missed out on many, immanent, relationship opportunities, because he was focused on the greener grass of the other side. This dream detailed, with multi-layered accuracy, precisely how and why John sabotaged his own circumstance and relationships.

However the dream's message was even more multifaceted. As the dream ends John sees the two girls disappearing into the distance. He is left alone and melancholy, which precisely represented his emotional state at the time of the dream. John's circumstance came about, not as much from making bad choices, as from his failure to make a choice. He sees his options disappearing, and his indecisiveness has left him emotionally impoverished.

This was a pivotal dream for John. As we peeled off the layers, it spoke in nuances that ultimately only John fully understood. Its multi-layered message helped him to more clearly fathom his own motivations (motivations which had previously been unconscious). He realized that his addictive and indecisive behaviors were compensating for his lack of self-worth – what Freud called an "*inferiority complex*". Using the self-awareness, culled from a deep analysis of this dream, John began to heal his life. Within six months he successfully overcame his double, alcohol/tobacco addiction, which led him to a greater sense of self-worth, and, in turn, redefined and restored his relationship with his brother and others. He also began to cultivate new relationships, based on making realistic, committed choices, and genuine connections, rather than artificial choices based on compensatory fantasy.

John's dream stands as an excellent example of the primacy of a dream. We see here the power of a single dream, which at first glance appeared nonsensical or insignificant, to open up a prodigious fountain of evocative insights that, finally, only John can fully appreciate. The ultimate meaning of this dream is accessible to John alone.

DREAM-SELFIE : THE MAGIC MIRROR

Even Freud, who, as a scientist, distained religion as a mere defense-mechanism, was quoted uncharacteristically: ***"The dream is the liberation of the spirit from the pressure of external nature, a detachment of the soul from the fetters of matter."*** (<u>Dream Psychology</u> 1921)

In the Vedic scriptures of ancient India, the illusionary world, which we experience with our senses, is represented by the goddess Maya, beautiful, illusive, impermanent and always changing. We are told that our entire universe is a dream, the dream of Vishnu resting on a giant, cosmic, multi-headed serpent; our lives are created by his dreaming. Such notions, of a psychic creation, whereby the universe is dreamt into existence from a divine mind, appear as a cornerstone of most mystical traditions.

In a very real sense, we each and all dream our own universe. Modern science fully supports the idea that our perception of the world is actually a conversion, of electromagnetic energy-waves and/or chemical reactions, into sensory experiences that occur in our brains. Technically speaking we are dreaming our lives – all that we think, feel and experience is generated within our brains, and, truly, what reality actually is, we have no idea. By making the invisible visible we participate in the creative process, but, if our perceived world emanates from a material reality, from where does our dream world arise? When I look at an apple various amplitudes of light entering my eye will produce the image, which I recognize as an apple, in my mind. When I dream of an apple, the recognizable image is there, but what is the source?

Just as we cannot look into our own eyes, we cannot directly apprehend the true source of being. In the Bible we are told that we cannot meet God face to face and live, "And He said: *'Thou canst not see My face, for man shall not see Me and live.'"* (Exodus 33:20); this implies that such an encounter would implode our consciousness and shatter the outer physical garment. Just so, by the laws of physics we cannot see our own faces directly; we cannot look directly into our own eyes except with the help of a mirror or camera. Just as with the physical body, our psyche cannot apprehend itself directly; some sort of reflective device is required to perceive an expression of our inner selves – *DREAMS*. Your dreaming mind provides the magic mirror that reflects images of your inner being – hence DREAM-SELFIE, the key to seeing ourselves.

The famous 17th century, French philosopher/scientist René Descartes famously stated: ***"Cogito ergo sum – I think, therefore I am"***. I've taken the liberty to slightly amend his assertion with my own quote: ***Cogito ergo sum ego somnia – I dream therefore I am.*** We cannot imagine a world without dreaming because dreams are the very fabric of our imagination, and our imagination is the very of fabric our lives.

Dream on!

APPENDIX
COLLECTION OF INSIGHTFUL
DREAM QUOTES

"Merrily, merrily, merrily life is but a dream" ~ Eliphalet Oram Lyte, 19th century American/English, Children's Teacher

"Dreams are a key to healing the soul." ~ Maimonides, 12th century Judeo/Spanish Physician and Philosopher

"You are the maker of the dream …Whatever you put into the dream must be what is in you. A dream is a message of yourself to yourself." ~ Fritz Perls 1893-1970 German-born, Psychiatrist and Psychotherapist

"Your vision will become clear only when you can look into your own heart." ~ Carl Jung, 20th century Psychologist and Psychoanalyst

"The interpretation of dreams is the royal road to a knowledge of the unconscious activities of the mind." ~ Sigmund Freud, 19th - 20th centuries, Austrian, Neurologist, Psychotherapist and founder of Psychoanalysis

"We each possess a lawless wild beast nature that peers out from sleep." ~ Socrates 5th century BCE. Greek, Philosopher

"Dreaming permits each and every one of us to be quietly and safely insane every night of our lives." ~ William Dement, 20th – 21st centuries, American Psychiatrist / Sleep Researcher

"I dream my painting and I paint my dream." ~ Vincent Willem van Gogh, 19th century, Dutch Painter

"I do not know whether I was then a man dreaming I was a butterfly, or whether I am now a butterfly dreaming I am a man." ~ Chuang Tzu, 4th- 3rd centuries BCE. Chinese, Taoist Teacher and Author.

"A dream which is not interpreted is like a letter which is not read" ~ Babylonian Talmud, 3[rd]century, Rabbinic

"Dreams are today's answers to tomorrow's questions" ~ Edgar Cayce, 19th – 20th centuries, American Clairvoyant and New Age Philosopher

"A dream is a microscope through which we look at the hidden occurrences in our soul." ~ Erich Fromm, 20th century, German/American, Social Psychologist

"The virtuous man contents himself with dreaming that which the wicked man does in actual life." ~ Sigmund Freud, <u>The Interpretation of Dreams</u>

"Without any help from the outside world (except of course its representation in memory), the brain is capable of creating such a remarkably faithful simulacrum of waking conscious reality that we are quite regularly fooled into taking it for the real thing – This must mean that the brain has all the hardware and software it needs to create a virtual reality of remarkable verisimilitude." ~ J. Allan Hobson, 20th/21st century, American Psychiatrist, <u>Consciousness</u> <u>1998.</u>

"If there is a prophet among you, I, the Lord, will appear to him in a dream, or will speak to him by means of a dream." ~ Biblical Book of Numbers, Moses.

"We are such stuff as dreams are made on, and our little life is rounded with a sleep." ~ William Shakespeare, 16th-17th centuries, English, Poet, Playwright and Actor

∾ ∾ ∾ END ∾ ∾ ∾

Only the dreamer knows the true meaning of their dreams

Michael Klein is a Dream Therapist based
in Toronto Canada where he is active as a,
writer, multi-media artist and teacher.

www.michaelklein.me